EDEN FADING

Michael Barnett

*To Mike,
I hope you enjoy this book!*

*Love, Brother
Mike Barnett*

PublishAmerica
Baltimore

© 2010 by Michael Barnett.
All rights reserved. No part of this book may be reproduced, stored in a retrieval system or transmitted in any form or by any means without the prior written permission of the publishers, except by a reviewer who may quote brief passages in a review to be printed in a newspaper, magazine or journal.

First printing

PublishAmerica has allowed this work to remain exactly as the author intended, verbatim, without editorial input.

Hardcover 978-1-4560-0226-8
Softcover 978-1-4560-0225-1
PUBLISHED BY PUBLISHAMERICA, LLLP
www.publishamerica.com
Baltimore

Printed in the United States of America

*Dedicated to Gilbert Barnett
Our unwavering Captain,
who now sails with our Lord.*

Special acknowledgements to
Glenda Barnett, my Mom.
Your strength in surviving all you did.
Your memories of details long past,
give this book substance.
And to
Gerald Barnett, my brother.
Without you prodding me to tell these stories,
they never would have been told.
And to
James and David Barnett: my brothers.
Your special insights, and memories,
adds depth to these pages.
And to
Michelle Barnett, my wife.
I cannot thank you enough for the time
you took in editing this work,
and keeping me honest.

Also, thanks to Larry Freeman
for the use of his 1956 Chevy in my author photo.

K Street

The approaching disaster pulls us; draws us, like ants to a flame.

Danny, Eddie, and Wayne, 1961

We arrive to a typical hazy summer day in Southern California, with the temperature hovering around the mid seventies. The air is redolent with the smells of eucalyptus trees and orange blossoms. Mixed with these obvious good smells is background smells, which are not so good…smells which are clearly part of this haze that surrounds us and envelops everything. It is August of 1961. We, the witnesses, are in the back yard of a small, light-green and white trim, two bedroom, one bath, and 800 square foot starter-house. There is a purple flowered bougainvillea covered lattice which takes up much of the back wall. A six foot cedar fence surrounds the back yard, with alternating baby-blue and crimson flowered hydrangeas planted every five feet along the back yard fences. At the back right of the yard is a large white playhouse, complete with front porch and railing, a working door, and two windows (not actual working windows, since there is no glass, or opening and closing mechanism—just square holes). At the pack left of the back yard is a one-car garage, painted the same light-green as the house. It is a normal lazy Monday morning, mostly quiet with husbands off at work, and their wives busily working on their chores. The occasional car or truck interrupts the silence, as it passes by out front (The muffled sound comes from the other end of a long tunnel…or other universe). A large walnut tree with massive branches that reach out to cover almost the entire back yard, and easily stands 100 feet tall is the centerpiece to this serene scene. It stands to the front right of the back yard, and blocks so much light, no matter how hard they try, grass will never grow under it. Underneath the full-sun-blocking branches of the walnut is a large handmade wooden picnic table (as is the playhouse), where two boys sit; one is three years old, and the other just under two. Both boys are wearing swimming trunks and T-shirts, and both are barefoot. They both have short blond hair, and hazel eyes like their Dad. They have the charm shared by young boys everywhere; they project purity and innocence, and have probably gathered here to talk about toys, or swimming pools, or maybe forts they can build where they can fight off imaginary Indians. The older boy suddenly hops up and walks quickly to a large homemade brick barbecue grill ten feet away, to retrieve something we cannot quite see.

We move closer to get a better look at this shiny object in Danny's hand and see that it is a beer bottle. He holds the bottle out to his younger brother, as he whispers something we can now just make out.

He says, "Drink this Wayne; it won't hurt you. Daddy was drinking it yesterday, and he's OK."

Wayne shakes his head stubbornly, with as much resolution as the older one trying to get him to take a drink. The older brother is relentless, and now switches his tactics.

He says, "Look! I will take a drink! Look! Watch Me! Watch, Wayne!"

His younger brother is now watching his hands he has folded on the table before him. The older brother tilts the bottle up and takes a big swallow. He once again holds the bottle out to Wayne, who is still adamantly shaking his head.

The older brother says, "Look! I'll drink some more. It doesn't hurt me!"

He takes another sip. The younger boy speaks in a voice remarkably quiet and timid.

Wayne says, "No Danny, Daddy told us not to touch those bottles, that they are bad for us."

Danny tries again, "This isn't bad, it's good, Mmmmmm…" he says with the most winning smile he can muster, and then takes another sip.

We can see what is happening. This is an old dance that both boys know well. Danny is the leader (by virtue of being the elder brother), and Wayne the follower (because he is the youngest). Wayne has made a valiant attempt at resistance, but we can see in his eyes that his strength is waning. Danny continues to hold out the bottle, but now he has begun to smile…just a little. We move in to get a better look. Something of importance is about to happen. We would like to be able to change what we see, but we are only witnesses. The boys are still frozen in their earlier poses, as the battle of wills goes on, and it is then that we smell something that immediately draws our attention. The smell is coming from the beer bottle, and it isn't beer. We quickly scan the Barbeque grill, and see what we are so afraid to see; perched high on the grill, but not high enough, is a metal can of lighter fluid. We frantically put the pieces together in our mind, and realize that Danny has taken an empty beer bottle (carelessly left there from a get-together the night before) and filled it with lighter fluid, to be used later. We immediately turn back just in time to see Wayne slowly reaching his hand out for the bottle. We can't stop it from happening, but we can't turn away either. Wayne now has the bottle and very slowly raises it to his lips. Immediately, he lowers the bottle.

Wayne says, "It smells bad."

This is more of a statement than an argument. The two brothers both know that this is a done deal.

Danny says, "Drink it," but he is no longer begging.

He says this with confidence he shares with all older brothers, whose sole purpose in life is to torment their younger brothers. Wayne nods in resignation then takes a sip. Wayne's hands fly to his mouth as his eyes open wide. This is quickly followed by a muffled cry as Wayne jumps to his feet. Something extraordinary happens then: Time swings back to its normal speed, which makes us realize that up until now, time has slowed. Time had no meaning, as is often the case when extreme events are taking place. Now, as Wayne stands next to the table and his cry turns into a wail, time catches up all at once. Wayne turns and sprints for the back door (on a course to get Mom), who is inside doing the laundry. We turn to look at Danny, and we see an intriguing thing happen. Like a *shape shifter*, he appears to change from a little monster back into a three-year old boy. Nothing changes physically, except for a drooping of the shoulders. The biggest change happens in his eyes: They go from willful and knowing to frightened and anxious. He just sits there on his side of the table, with his hands gently folded on his lap, waiting for his Mom to come out and punish him. He is well accustomed, it seems, with the, "break a rule, get punished" cycle. He has obviously traveled this road before.

For a while, his Mom doesn't come. He is both grateful and a little confused by this. Finally, after what seems like an eternity, he hears the sound of a siren far off. The siren grows louder and more insistent until it dies altogether out on the front street. Danny knows that sound from TV shows and it exhilarates him. Within a few short minutes, the back door opens and slams shut. A very petite blond-haired, blue-eyed woman who seems much too young to be the mother of these children rounds the corner at a fast walk. She is wearing a pair of white pedal-pusher slacks, sandals, and a loose multicolored blouse. Danny is particularly glad he thought to drop the beer bottle (filled with the damning lighter fluid) under the table. He is also aware that during his handling of the bottle (and the drinking of the contents), quite a bit of the fluid spilled on the picnic table in front of him, and his clothes. Not much he can do about that. He sits up straight and watches his Mom as she draws up, then kneels down next to him.

"Danny, an ambulance is here to get Wayne and take him to the hospital", she says.

"Your brother said he drank some of the lighter fluid in the white can, the poison your Dad told you to stay away from", she concludes.

Mom's nose picks up the overpowering smell of lighter fluid. She turns to look at the lighter fluid can on the top of the barbecue grill and wonders how Wayne was able to reach it in the first place. Danny is dismayed to know that his brother discovered his deception of hiding the lighter fluid in the beer bottle. Mom now leans forward to smell his breath.

She says, "Danny, did you drink any of the lighter fluid?"

Amazed that she doesn't smell the lighter fluid on his breath, he answers,

"No Mommy, I didn't drink anything."

His Mom stares into his eyes for a moment longer, searching for the lie, and decides he is telling the truth. He realizes he was saved by the strong smell of lighter fluid on his clothes and table. His Mom now nods her head.

She says, "I called Mrs. Reyes to come and take you and Eddie to her house, while I go to the hospital in the ambulance with Wayne, OK?"

Danny is starting to feel better about how things have turned out. He nods his head, stands up and walks with his Mom back towards the house.

We follow these two up the back steps on to the back porch, through the laundry room, then through the kitchen and Dining room, and into the front living room where two paramedics are loading Wayne on to a gurney. Mrs. Reyes is standing there holding a baby in her arms who is screaming like a banshee, while he holds out his arms for Mom. Meet Eddie, the third child.

"Maria: thank you again for coming so quickly," Mom says.

Maria reaches out with her free arm and hugs Mom, then whispers intently as she faces her,

"Jean, we are friends! This is what friends do. You take care of Wayne. I will watch Danny and little Eddie. You go. We'll be fine."

Mom says, "Let me get a bag for Eddie together real quick; diapers, clothes, bottles."

As the two Paramedic's give each other a look of impatience, which both women see clearly,

Maria says, "No, I'll get everything I need. You don't worry about that. Now go and be with your Son."

The paramedics quickly wheel Wayne out to the waiting ambulance (a long bright-white 1960 Miller Meteor Cadillac, with the characteristic "hump on top"), where Mom climbs in, then off they go. Danny stands together with Mrs. Reyes, as his Mom and brother speed away, the siren wailing its crazy-mournful cry. The ambulance mesmerizes Danny, by how beautiful and breathtaking it is.

2

We know that Wayne is cared for. Our interests lie with Danny, so we follow him. Eddie continues to scream despite Maria's best efforts to distract him with her keys. Strangely, Danny is not bothered by this piercing and strangely siren-like wailing. After Maria packs a bag with Eddie's things, and gets him loaded up in the stroller, she takes hold of Danny's hand then off they go out the door to her house. Once they get there, she calls out to her husband.

She yells, "Humberto, come here quick, please."

He enters from the other room, and Maria fills him in on what happened. Humberto listens quietly and says a silent prayer when she finishes; barely moving his lips as he does so. He then crosses himself and takes a still-screaming Eddie from Maria's arms. Danny watches all of this impassively, then moves to the couch and flops down, while Humberto sets Eddie in a crib that Maria keeps for her sister's kids when they come to visit. Maria turns the black and white TV on for Danny and switches quickly through the three available channels until she reaches *Alvin and the Chipmunks*. With Danny fully engaged, Maria returns to Eddie to see what he needs. After a quick diaper change, his crying finally stops. Maria is behind on chores, so she picks up clutter and finishes sweeping her floors.

"Poor kid...watching something like that happen to your little brother," she thinks.

Every time she walks by Danny she glances his way, to make sure he is doing OK. On her third pass by, she looks at Danny much more carefully. She looks at him again. Something doesn't feel right. Danny is much too subdued and usually has much more energy. She sees that his skin is pale, and his mouth is hanging open. On closer inspection, she sees his eyes are glazed.

She asks him, "Danny, Honey, are you OK? You don't look well."

Maria sits down next to Danny on the couch and immediately the smell of lighter fluid assaults her. She chastises herself for not changing his clothes first, before bringing the kids over here. What was she thinking? All people have moments of enlightenment in their lives, maybe just one, and now Maria has one that likely saves Danny's life.

She asks, "Danny, did you drink any of the poison Wayne drank?"

Danny is shaking his head no. After all, once you tell a lie, there's no going back. Maria has an unusually strong feeling about this.

She asks again, "Danny, you won't get in trouble Honey if you tell me the truth. If you have been poisoned, I need to take you to the hospital."

Danny decides to come clean, because he can tell she won't give up. He draws in a big breath, to tell her more, and then he burps...not a little one either. Immediately a large amount of lethal gas escapes his mouth and shocks Maria so much she leans back in surprise. She now fully understands that Danny is much sicker than she or anyone else thought. Surprising Danny, she picks him up into her arms, and then yells for Humberto. He walks in from the kitchen as she tells him she has to take Danny to the hospital right now. Maria gives out instructions for taking care of Eddie (Who, wonder of wonders, has started screaming again). Maria doesn't wait for an acknowledgement from Humberto, but heads out the door, with Danny still in her arms, depositing him in the spacious back seat of their old green 1949 Plymouth 4-door sedan.

Once Maria sits behind the wheel, a previously quiet Danny asks,

"Don't I get an ambulance too? Why do I have to go in a car?"

She looks at him as she starts the car, then answers,

"We don't have time Honey. We're going to the hospital now."

In the rearview mirror, she sees a look on Danny's face that gives her the chills. For just a few seconds, she sees extreme rage on the boys face; or what her husband calls, 'A look that can kill'. Then, just as quickly his entire countenance switches to no emotion at all. A strange cocking of his head accompanies this blank face, as if he has just heard some sound far off, and trying to find it. This lack of emotion on his face, this total departure from anything human, especially in one so young, remind Maria of the look on Vincent Price's face in that movie her husband took her to see at the drive-in last year…something about a pit. It doesn't matter. That was the same look.

She whispers, "¡Aye, Dios Mio! Ayúdeme Jesús."

She quickly makes the sign of the cross as she stares once more at the boy in the back seat.

"He's very sick. I'm just imagining things. That's all," she thinks.

Maria speeds towards the hospital, being just careful enough to keep from having an accident, and eager to get out of this car. Against her better judgment, Maria routinely glances at Danny and sees the same vacant look on his face. The inside of the car is eerily quiet, except for a soft and mournful tune coming from the radio; "Crazy," by Patsy Cline.

In the back seat, Danny sits and broods. He knows he is sick, but he is angry too. Danny obsesses with the idea that his brother got to go to the hospital in an ambulance; that he got to travel in style, with the siren at full volume. On the other hand, *he* has to make the same trip to the hospital in a car; a dull and drab (and quiet), car. Nobody will look at him as he speeds by. He doesn't even get to hear a siren like riding in an ambulance. Danny thinks of his brother a lot. He always has, but, not in the way you may think. His thoughts are darker than any three-year-old has any business thinking. He does not feel sorry for Wayne, as he seems incapable of that emotion. Danny's thoughts are much more primitive and basic.

Danny thinks, "How do I kill him next time?"

The Doctor

We are now in a waiting room. It is small and has uncomfortable plastic chairs. There are two artificial plants; one at each diagonal end. The walls are bright white, and the floor is light-grey linoleum, which is somehow not made any brighter by some exceptionally bright fluorescent lights above, which removes all possibility of shadows. There was no attempt to improve on the desolate, moonscape-like surroundings; whose purpose should have made families feel more comfortable. There are a few lonely, unframed, and uninteresting paintings; which are too small for the large white walls on which they hang. They do the opposite of the intention, by drawing attention to the stark nature of these walls. There is nothing pleasant or comforting here, to make a person think they are any place other than "The place" where your loved ones are suffering or dying on the other side of these walls. There is the overwhelming smell of stale cigarette smoke mixed with that of disinfectant, and hints of other smell common to hospitals which do not warrant discussing. We see that most of the people here are smoking. Scatterings of coffee cups lay on tables, floor, and chairs, some empty, some not, some warm, some not. We walk further into the room, all the way to the back, and we see some old friends. Mom is sitting on the edge of her chair, leaning forward, with her elbows on her knees and her forehead resting on her hands. On her right-hand side is Maria, who is extremely busy worrying at a hangnail (it has become her sole concern). To Mom's left, is a new person, we have not yet. He is unusually tall and exceptionally strong, with short black hair, and some of the largest arms we have ever seen. He is wearing a white T-shirt, blue jeans (with the bottoms rolled up to high-water level), and tennis shoes. His massive arms are now folded, and he is shaking his head in an exaggerated fashion; like a Shakespearean Actor who needs to be seen by people far from the stage. We see that this man is highly animated in many ways; with expansive arm movements, and high-set bushy-black eye brows which jump up and down to match his full range of facial expressions. His emotions quickly run through; anger, disbelief, amazement, puzzlement, disillusionment, disappointment, and impatience. This person is Dad, and we quickly surmise, does not believe in whispering, or being inconspicuous…it is not in his nature. He believes that what he says is always what people want, or need to hear.

He is currently berating Mom, "I have to work! I can't leave work every time you fail to watch your children! We need every penny I make. Do you want to get me fired? Do you want us to live on the street?"

His rage is barely contained, but nobody else in the waiting room dares to step in to defend Mom. He is one of those rare people who can command attention even when a person strives mightily to ignore him entirely. We glance around the waiting room and see most people watching this show with a mixture of both fascination and fear. This Man knows he scares people. Oh yes, he has always known this…but he doesn't understand how much. Mom, who has been analyzing the patterns on the linoleum between her knees, finally looks up.

She says, "You know how they *are*. I turn my back for two seconds, and they're gone! One minute they're watching TV, the next minute they're gone! They always wake up early before we get up. You know that! They are always so quiet when they are getting into trouble. How can I keep an eye on them every minute of the day? I have Eddie to watch after too you know!"

Here, Mom pauses. What she almost said—and is genuinely glad she didn't—was that he is never around to help with the kids. Even when he is there, he isn't. She turns and looks up at the man

She says, "Buck, please try to understand, I do try to keep an eye on them. I'm convinced that Danny is constantly planning their next mischief."

Dad cuts her off, "You're not listening! What the hell are you saying? Planning? Danny is three years old. He's just a little kid! Just like any kid, he needs supervision, which obviously you aren't providing. You're dumber than a box of rocks."

Dad is now shaking his head and making his "Disappointed" face while Mom looks off with unveiled frustration. She is struggling with how she can explain this to her husband. She knows this is a battle she can't win, so she decides to keep quiet. Just as Dad turns towards Mom to say something else,

"Walker!"

We glance up to see a doctor standing in the entrance to the waiting room, chart in hand, surveying the room. The traditional white Doctor's coat adorns him (double-breasted Chinese collar, made popular by Psychiatrists before doctor's adopted it), with dark slacks, and black shoes. A stethoscope hangs from his neck, and some writing instruments are in a single pocket. A name tag too small to see from here finishes off his outfit. He has medium length blond hair. He wears a pair of black horn-rimmed glasses, is no taller than Mom, who is just over 5' 4", and probably weighs no more than most 14-year-old boys. He has a few wrinkles around his eyes and across his forehead, but his age is difficult to determine. He looks down at the chart in his hand.

He says, "The family of Danny and Wayne Walker?"

Mom raises her hand and says, "Here we are."

The parents stand and move quickly to where the doctor stands.

Before they can reach him, the doctor says, "Follow me please," and leads them away down the hall.

Dad, irritated that Mom is walking ahead of him, passes her. We must hasten to catch up, and do so, just as the doctor is leading the couple into a private office.

As we all enter the office, the doctor moves around a large desk, taking a seat in a large wooden desk chair. The office is spacious, with bookshelves packed with hardcover books taking up two of the walls, and a wall to wall window behind the desk. A large dark-stained oak desk dominates the room, leaving two matching straight-backed visitor chairs facing the front of the desk. The one bare wall is entirely covered with diplomas and certificates; all framed and carefully arranged. There is the smell of old libraries mingled with Old Spice aftershave. The parents stand uncomfortably in the doorway as the doctor finally waves them over almost dismissively with a hand movement reminding us of something done by royalty.

He says, "Please...sit. Oh, and close the door."

Mom and Dad sit in the visitor's chairs; which are as uncomfortable as the plastic ones in the waiting room. The doctor says nothing for an extraordinarily long and anxious time, as he leans forward studying the chart, constantly flipping noisily through the pages. We see a large emerald and gold decorated plaque prominently displayed on the desk which reads, "Doctor Philip Savage, Chief of Staff."

The parents look at each other with mounting anxiety. Finally, the doctor looks up from his chart.

He says, "I am Doctor Savage; Chief of Staff of our lovely hospital here."

He sits up straighter and juts out his chin as he says this. Dad now speaks up in a deep, booming voice louder than is necessary for this small office.

"What's this all about?"

Mom says, "How are the boys? Are they OK?"

"Yes, yes, they're fine. We'll get to that in a minute."

This interruption causes a flash of irritation to visit the doctor's face. He flips to the back page of his chart, takes a moment to read something, and then looks up.

He says, "Just two days ago...Saturday, both boys were here early afternoon, and had their stomachs' pumped of...let's see...an overdose of Ex-Lax?"

Both parents nod their heads, but then Dad glances at Mom and shakes his head in a disapproving way; reminding her, no doubt, of her earlier perceived transgressions.

Doctor Savage continues, "Now today, Monday, two days later…"

He glances at his watch, "almost the same time…"

He looks up and holds eye contact with first Dad and then Mom for exactly two seconds each. The look on the doctor's face is one of amusement, like this is a play or skit, done for his pleasure only.

The Doctor continues, "So, where were we? Oh yes, today your boys come in, but separate this time. I'm sure there is an interesting story, for that…a far out explanation."

This is not a question to hear the story, but a statement of fact, said in such a way that the parents understand the doctor has no interest in an answer. The doctor is trying to act younger with the parents; to speak their language, but he doesn't have a handle on it.

The Doctor goes on, "Anyway, Wayne comes in right after lunch, and Danny follows about a half hour later. Both had their stomachs' pumped…again."

He shakes his head as if disgusted, and continues, "The difference this time is that both boys drank lighter fluid, a highly flammable liquid that is easily aspirated into the lungs. Fearing chemical pneumonia, methanol poisoning, and scarring to the lung tissue, x-ray's to both boys' lungs was done. Kind of a drag…"

Here the doctor pauses to let what he has already said take effect. Here, is a doctor who loves his job (not just the fixing and healing of patients), but also being the harbinger of news, both good and bad. He studies the faces of these young parents with a calculated intensity, and we can see that he has succeeded in worrying Mom. Dad has more of a look of curiosity than fear or worry.

The Doctor goes on, "Let's see, I have the X-ray results…I always get these mixed up."

He gives his biggest and brightest, award-winning smile; which is so inappropriate for the moment that both parents (unaware they are doing so), tilt their heads to the left, and frown in the same way. The Doctor doesn't register this reaction (he is on a roll); he still has some terrific stuff to deliver.

He wastes no time in continuing, "Wayne's lungs are OK, nothing to worry about there…so far. Danny, however, has a small spot on his right lung. This is not necessarily a problem, but we will need to keep an eye on him for a while. Both boys may develop pneumonia. Unfortunately, there are many people who die from this type of poisoning each year, and some of the more pronounced symptoms don't manifest until several hours or days later. Some of the symptoms are; trouble breathing, headaches, problems focusing, acute coughing, trouble keeping their balance when walking, etc."

Dad is frowning again, and now speaks up, "You could have told us all of this in the waiting room, or in the hallway, for that matter. Why did you bring us here?"

The doctor studies Dad for a few seconds as if trying to make a decision.

He responds, "Why indeed! I brought you to my office because of what I have to say. I felt you would appreciate the message delivered in private. I'm trying to decide whether I should call the police. They will probably engage social services, for willful neglect resulting in injury to a child…children. This is very messy business. You may lose your children. This is all so tragic."

Mom is the first to answer this time, "What? We do not neglect our children! These were just accidents!"

Tears are now streaming down Mom's face, as she turns to her husband for help. Dad is already leaning forward.

He says, "These were accidents that will not happen again! I can promise you that!"

Dad now favors Mom with his look of disappointment, and an additional rolling of his eyes. This looks to be one of his favorite weapons in his arsenal, and he does this to convey to the doctor (not just Mom), that he is a man in charge, he will keep Mom in line, and of that the doctor has no worries.

Dad again looks at the Doctor, and with all of his powers of persuasion says, "Our boys are well taken care of. We live in a nice house. The boys are well-fed and provided for. I know how this all looks, but we promise our boys will never be in here again, for any reason."

Mom and Dad are staring at the Doctor with hope, while feeling as they are dangling over a precipice with no safe way back to safety. The doctor again, for dramatic purposes perhaps, pauses as if making a monumental decision that will shape the future of the world. Doctor Savage is absently rubbing his chin with his thumb and forefinger of his left hand, and twirling a pen in his right as he leans back in his chair and stares out the window; as if there is a beautiful mountain landscape out there instead of just a brick wall. After 30 seconds (But to the Walker's it seems like years), Doctor Savage leans forward suddenly, startling both parents, and takes a deep breath.

He says, "What to do? What to do? I will *not* call the police…this time."

Both parents visibly relax by leaning back in their chairs, and loosening their tight grips on their arm rests; letting out a sigh as they do so that neither is aware of.

The doctor goes on, "We will keep both children here for observation overnight to make sure there are no unexpected effects from the poisoning. Consider yourselves very lucky that your children are not now on life support, or dead. However, over the course of the next 24 hours, who can say for certain?"

We see by the exaggerated sad smile on the doctor's face along with the raising of the arms, palms up, to let them know it's out of his hands. This is the part of the speech he loves; the part where he gets to first convict, then pardon this young couple's actions. Doctor Savage hops up out of his chair and quickly moves past the parents to the door, startling them both.

Before opening it, he adds, "You *will* pay more attention to your children now, won't you? After all, just a call from me to the police…I would hate to see a pattern developing here."

Both parents nod their heads as they answer in the affirmative because this is the answer the doctor is expecting. Doctor Savage looks at them intently for a few moments more, then opens the door as the young couple come to their feet to follow him out into the hall.

He says, "Oh, I almost forgot. Within the next hour, your boys will be out of recovery, and a nurse will come and find you in the waiting room to take you to your boy's room. You two, take care of those boys. Groovy, you two take it easy."

With this final exclamation, the doctor leans over to close his office door, and then quickly heads down the hallway, to some new destination. As he reaches full stride, he can be heard whistling the song from the old movie with the same name, "The High and the Mighty."

Running Amok

53 minutes later, we are now walking slightly behind Mom and Dad, who are in turn, following an older nurse (name tag says, Nurse Rench), complete with bouffant hairdo, and the nurses' white cap with black stripe perched precariously on top of all that hair. She also has a white dress, white hose, and white shoes. When we arrived here at the hospital with Mrs. Reyes and Danny, we saw many nurses dressed like this, but also wearing navy-blue capes over their shoulders walking to and from the hospital. Despite the nurses' advanced age, she is walking at such a rapid pace that only Dad, with his long legs has no problem keeping up. Poor Mom is constantly shifting between walk-run-walk-run, just to keep pace. They have just stepped off the elevator, which has taken them up to the second floor, and are walking to the last room on the longest wing of the hospital (which they don't register now), is decided by design, in trying to isolate the young boys from the general population. The same white motif exists here, as it did on the first floor. Except now there are black floors, and matching black paint that goes halfway up the walls (this suggests to Mom and Dad that the hospital "powers that be", finally got fed up with trying to keep the floor and walls sparkling white-clean, so decided to "go with it"). The hint of body smells downstairs, are no longer a hint here; they are a real and attention-demanding presence. As they pass each room, and a new offensive smell assaults them, Mom and Dad realize they have started breathing through their mouths, and are holding their breaths when it gets too bad. They finally get to the last doorway on the left, room 222 and enter without pausing. We ftlineenter right behind them and see that both boys are in their own beds and are being hovered over by another nurse (her name tag reads, Nurse Thompson). She is much younger than their escort, Nurse Rench. Both nurses confer in private for a few moments, and Nurse Thompson leaves. We turn our attention back to the boys and see that they are unusually quiet and still. This behavior is only unusual in the very young. Mom goes to Wayne's bed where she leans over him and kisses his forehead while taking his hand.

Mom says, "How're you feeling honey? Feeling better?"

Wayne nods and says, "Huh-huh. I'm OK Mommy."

Dad has drifted over to Danny.

He says, "Hi Son, you gave your Mom and Dad quite a scare. I guess you know you're in trouble over this, but we'll talk about that later."

Mom says, "Buck, don't talk about that now. We're just thankful that you two are OK, aren't we Dad?"

Dad says, "Of course, I am, of course I care!"

He says this with a brief frown, and we can see him struggling not to react too harshly at this perceived slight. Mom stands up and now goes to Danny, repeating the same comforting words she used with Wayne and getting a similar response. After a few moments Mom stands, then backs up to the foot of the beds, so she can look at both boys.

She says, "Mommy and Daddy were very worried about you guys. We love you both very much, and don't want you doing these things any more. OK?"

Both boys nod. Dad is standing quietly, and now, not so stealthily, sneaks a look at his watch.

He says, "Well Sons, it's getting late. I missed my lunch because of you…, uh, I mean because of this, so Mom and I need to go get something to eat. We'll be back later, OK?"

Again, there are nods in unison. Both boys are so exhausted from their ordeal; they will sleep the whole time. Both parents take turns with each son, Mom kissing them on the cheeks, and Dad putting his hand on their shoulders with words of encouragement. They now walk to the door, and one look at Mom's face says she would rather stay with the boys, but goes along with her husband. One more round of goodbyes and the parents move out into the hallway, where they briefly chat with the nurse before leaving. We decide to stay with the boys and take our invisible seats, settling in for a long wait.

We don't have to wait long, as the parents haven't even boarded the elevator yet when Danny slips out of his bed and then stands over Wayne, who is still lying remarkably still under his covers. Danny is whispering again, in that fast paced, frenetic way we have already heard him use. He is like an old-fashioned "Hell-fire and brimstone" Preacher; trying with all his strength to get through to his flock of one… Wayne. Like a preachers' congregation, Wayne is listening intently to every word which he hears. Curiosity has overcome us, and we now rise and move to Danny's side to strain to hear what he is saying. What we hear first shocks us, then, amazes us.

Danny says, "Wayne, this is a fun place. We can do what we want. We can run and play, because Mommy and Daddy aren't here. This is like a big playground!"

Wayne says while shaking his head, "We'll get in trouble. Those white people will make us in trouble. I don't feel good anyway."

This is a long sentence for Wayne, who usually lets Danny do the talking and decision-making for both. Also, interestingly enough, Danny and Wayne know each other perfectly (Unusual for siblings of three and one and a half). Danny knows that what Wayne calls "White people" are simply the hospital workers…the nurses and doctors. Danny never laughs at Wayne, or ridicules him. He has no need to feel superior; he has no sense of humor. Danny, it seems is an extremely complicated three-year-old. One minute he is trying to kill his brother, the next minute partnering with him for some great adventure.

Danny now employs a practiced strategy and says, "OK Wayne, I will go play and I won't get in trouble. You just stay here all by yourself."

Monsters have many faces, and this one is no different. This little boy knows how to prey on (and how to exploit) the weaknesses of his younger brother. Wayne lets out a cry of desperation.

Wayne says, "No, I don't want to be alone. Please don't leave me."

He says this last sentence with such sorrow and heartbreak, we can barely watch. When his mouth starts to tremble, and the tears begin to run, we wish we could forfeit our responsibility of being only witnesses. We look to Danny, expecting to see guilt or sadness, or discomfort at doing this to his younger brother, but see nothing. No emotion is on his face at all. His expression is that of a scientist dissecting some specimen with a scalpel and skill. Danny now holds out his hand for Wayne to take. Once again, we have an agreement to do what the older brother wants. This whole conversation happens quickly, and now, more quickly yet, Danny leads Wayne to the doorway where they pause for just a moment, then out the door they go. What happens next is a blur. Suffice it to say that they move quickly, and are truly quick for their ages. There is a lot of running, and a lot of screeching. Danny and Wayne don't just keep to the hallways, but enter rooms in a haphazard way, grabbing in flight, whatever catches their interest; band-aids, tape, and gauze pads are just a few. The boys escape the "White people" for a while, but Wayne is the first to be caught, then after a few more minutes, Danny is also caught. So much disruption in such a short time; kids of all ages are yelling, and walking (but mostly running) out into the hallways wondering what just happened. Nurses are all pooling around these kids and escorting them back to their beds, with comforting words and promises of peace and quiet, and call buzzers have assembled into a crazy non-rhythmical cacophony. The boys, to their credit, do not put up any resistance to delay the capture. Maybe it's because there are now two nurses escorting the boys back to their beds. Nurse Rench, who we met earlier takes the lead, and kneels in front of them, looking as serious as she can.

She says, "You boys are very sick. You are to stay in those beds. You are not to move from those beds for any reason. You have disturbed most of the patients on this floor, and we will *not* stand for it. Do I make myself clear?"

Both boys nod in the right places. They look very much subdued, so Nurse Rench feels that her point is made. Both nurses leave, and the door is now closed. Perhaps they think this will provide a satisfactory impediment to any shenanigans. The nurses have a handicap; they do not frighten the boys like their father does. Within a few minutes, the boys are at the door, listening for any sound beyond. Once satisfied, off they go again.

It is just after seven that evening, and Mom and Dad are hurrying from the elevator, eager to visit their boys. As they come abreast of the Nurses Station, Nurse Rench, who has watched for them, stands quickly and meets them in the hallway.

She says, "Excuse me, Mr. and Mrs. Walker? Can I have a word please?"

"Yes," they both respond in unison.

"I don't want to upset you, but we had some trouble with your Son's while …"

"What?" Mom says too loudly. Then lower, "What happened?"

Mom has a worried look on her face.

Realizing that the parents think their children have taken a turn for the worse, Nurse Rench now says,

"I'm sorry. I didn't mean to imply that your children have any physical problems. What I am trying to prepare you for is what you are about to see. I want to explain it to you before you go in and see your children. You must understand, or what you see will make no sense at all. Do you see what I'm saying?"

Mom and Dad look at each other with astonishment, and they slowly turn back to her.

Dad says, "What happened?"

He says it in a way that is different from how Mom said it earlier. He says it in a tone caused by the dawning realization that once again, his boys, absurd as it sounds, have gotten into trouble. Nurse Rench begins to tell her story. It isn't particularly long, but it does have some intriguing developments. She explains about the running in the hallway, the capture, the scolding, the shut door. She then mentions that, within a few minutes, the boys were running around screaming and laughing again. This is followed by re-capture, and re-imprisonment in their room, but this time, not in their beds. She now takes a slight detour to explain how Nurses have jobs to do, and can't have young boys running around disturbing the patients, and keeping the nurses from doing their jobs. She also adds how terrible it would be if the boys were to find the exits or the elevators. Heaven forbid if that had happened. Dad is tiring of this story and wants to see for himself.

Dad says, "I'm going to go see my Son's."

He turns and walks away quickly, with Mom right after him. The nurse is running to catch up, and is visibly exasperated by at her failure to explain herself. Once we get to the open door and peer in, we see Mom and Dad standing frozen in the entrance to the room, with the nurse standing right behind. To their left, two twin beds are pushed together to make room for two cribs in the opposite corner. Each boy is standing in his own crib, with hands gripping the bars in jailhouse fashion. Neither boy is crying, but they are sad and pathetic looking. Tied around a single ankle of each boy is a tie-down strap. The other ends of the straps tie to the cribs. The last thing the parents notice is that both boys are wearing diapers. Before either parent overcomes their surprise to start talking, the nurse senses her chance to try to diffuse this situation.

She says, "The second time they went running in the hallways, Doctor Johnson, who is our On-duty doctor tonight, said that if we didn't do something about your boys, he would be forced to put them under fulltime guard. One of the younger nurses came up with the idea of putting them in the cribs, to keep them from getting out…brilliant, really. That way, we could go about our duties and not waste a nurse on guard-duty. That didn't work either."

Nurse Rench says this last sentence with a combination of exhausted whine, and total exasperation.

Mom says just two words, "The straps."

You can tell she is trying desperately to understand what she is seeing.

Nurse Rench says, "Well, your kids are like little monkeys, that's what they are. I've never seen anything like it. They were out of their cribs in no time, and running the halls again. After another chase, we caught them, but I have to tell you, we have a lot of very upset patients now…and staff members for that matter."

Dad responds, "I understand about the crib and the straps. I probably would have done the same thing myself. What's the deal with the diapers? Danny's been out of diapers for?"

"Two years," Mom answers.

Nurse Rench continues, "Well, we don't know why…maybe it's the stress of their day, or the poison they ingested…both boys defecated in their pants."

Dad shakes his head in a bewildered, head-down manner like he would rather be any place else but here. Mom moves to Wayne and bends over the crib to hug him tight for a few moments. She then moves to Danny and does the same. Again, the opposing facts between what we see and what we *know* confuses us. Looking at these sick little faces now, we cannot reconcile their current behavior with that of the little hellions running about earlier. We are confident these thoughts are running through the minds of Mom and Dad as well, but unlike the extreme reactions of the hospital people, theirs is also tempered by weathering so many such outbursts before. Mom and Dad grab the two plastic chairs (imagine that, plastic!) stacked near the beds over in front of the cribs and settle down to be with their children before visiting time is over and they leave. We don't listen in this time. This time is for them, and we respect that, so we retreat out the door.

It is just after nine the next morning, and Mom and Dad arrive back at Danny and Wayne's room. They have stopped for breakfast on the way, and are somewhat well rested considering a restless night for Mom because of constant thoughts of what almost happened to her babies. Dad woke often too, because Mom woke him every time she got up to get something to drink, or to take a walk, or just stare out the windows in the front room. As soon as they enter the room, they realize that one element has changed. Instead of the loose straps attached to each child's leg, the straps are much tighter now. In fact, the cinched straps are so tight to the rails each boy's ankles are right up against them. The looks on Mom and Dad's faces show that they are now outraged at this unexpected development. The parents discussed over breakfast how both boys had learned their lesson, and are probably back in their beds and behaving themselves. Both boys have also assumed their original positions as inmates of this hospital-prison. Before the parents have a chance to respond, a voice speaks up from behind them.

"They're a handful."

Oddly enough, this is said with admiration from a young nurse who walks up next to Mom and Dad.

The nurse continues, "Hello, I'm Joanna, Sorry, Nurse Peters. I took over for the night nurse, Nurse Rench, this morning."

Mom says, "Hello Joanna."

This brings a smile to Joanna's face. She briefly squeezes Mom's hand, as a show of solidarity.

Joanna says, "Your boys were creating quite a spectacle last night. You know we tied them down with straps to their cribs?"

There are simultaneous nods from both Mom and Dad.

Joanna continues, "Well, it seems they figured out how to climb and stand on top of the rails, then jump off head first ..."

"What!" Mom yells as she runs over to kneel in front of the cribs. She looks closely at each child, expecting to see some bumps and bruises on each boy, but finds nothing. She spins on the balls of her feet, keeping one hand on the closest crib for stability.

She says, "I don't understand. How could they have jumped headfirst?"

"They Couldn't!" Dad adds, "That's impossible."

Already, Dad's subsequent statement is weaker. Doubt based on experience, doubt from seeing his kids do the unbelievable over and over, intrude.

Joanna, again with admiration in her voice goes on "When I came on shift at six, the night nurse briefed me on all patients, and she spent a long time talking about all the mischief your boys got into. All of a sudden, we hear one of the Patient Care Technicians scream from down here. We arrived here at a run, convinced that your boys had finally succeeded in hurting themselves, look in and are just in time to see the older boy dive off the top of the crib head first with arms at his side. I don't think that is normal."

Mom and Dad both favor her with identical looks of stunned disbelief, so she continues,

"So, he's falling, and all three of us are holding our breath, waiting for his head to hit. But no more than an inch from the floor, the strap around his ankle pulls tight, and he bounces back up the other way. I mean, I was so stoked."

Here, she stops talking as she stares off with a look that says she is enjoying these memories immensely.

Just as the parents are about to say something again, Joanna continues with a rush, "It was the damnedest thing I have ever seen in my life. He had no fear at all, just jumped right off and when he stopped swinging, grabbed a hold of the bars and pulled himself back up to the top. They are very strong for kids so young. "

Again the stare, but this time the parents just wait it out.

Finally, she adds, "You ever hear of an island in the south pacific called Pentecostal, or something like that?"

Again a pause, but not as long this time, "Back when I was a junior in High School, we saw this film about natives of Pentecostal Island. They climb handmade bamboo towers that are over 100 feet high. Then they tie a vine to their ankle, and then they just jump off head first. They want to see how close they can get to the ground without hitting their heads. Did your boys ever see that video, or watch a movie or something that showed them how to do that?"

Dad is shaking his head as he listens to the question,

He says, "No, I have never heard of that, and I know we have never seen anything like that."

Dad hesitates, frowns, then turns to Joanna and says,

"Wait, you said their heads? Both boys were jumping?"

Shock is dawning on Mom and Dad's faces.

She says, "No, that can't be possible. Wayne is too young, not as bold or fearless as Danny, and you're right, we didn't think he was as strong as Danny."

Joanna is shaking her head and says,

We didn't see Wayne jump, but the tech did. She said she watched both boys for a while as each boy took turns diving off, then climb back up, then jump off again. She said that the only reason she screamed was Danny jumped way out away from the crib, then swung back and slammed into the crib pretty hard."

All three adults stare at the boys silently. The boys stare right back with the poker-face looks of the prisoners they are.

Now in a softer voice, Joanna says, "How do you think they know how to do that? How could they know their heads wouldn't hit the floor?"

She says this last with the dawning realization of someone hyped up on adrenalin after a close-call with the Angel of Death, only to re-discover her mortality. With these new insights, a gloomy mood replaces Joanna's previous good cheer. She is unaccustomed to gloomy moods. Joanna finally understands what 'Someone walking over your grave' means; that has just happened to her. She says her goodbyes, reminding the parents she can be reached by buzzer. She heads off to try to analyze these new thoughts. Joanna may never understand these boys, but that's OK, the parents have ways to go on that, as well. Both parents have their suspicions that if they can understand the enigma that is Danny, understanding Wayne will be easier. We now leave the parents with their thoughts, and worries, and leave them for some private time with their boys. Yes, these boys are monsters, but they are their monsters.

Doctor Walberg visits several hours later and gives the boys a checkup. He checks their heart rates, blood pressure, pupil dilation test, and listening to the Boy's lungs as they breathe deep. Afterwards, the parents are given the standard admonishment about not letting children have access to hazardous chemicals and liquids, and always watch them, etcetera. Once the doctor feels he has satisfactorily saved another family from destroying itself, he signs the discharge papers, and they are all ready to go. Mom excuses herself and walks over to the nurse's station. She spies Joanna walking down the other hall.

Mom asks her, "Joanna, can I have a minute of your time?"

"Of course," she says as she changes direction and comes over to meet Mom.

Once Joanna is close, Mom whispers, "I can't believe I'm asking you this, but, can I somehow get two sets of those tie-down straps you used on my boys?"

Joanna does not understand this request.

She asks, "Why would you need those?"

Mom, a little more confident now, continues,

"You saw what trouble my boys get into. It doesn't take long for it to happen either. At home, they like to get out of their beds during the night, or get up real early, and get into things. Nothing is off-limits. First, they eat a whole box of Ex-lax, now they drink lighter fluid. There's no telling what they'll get into next. I know they can still get up to no good during the day when they're running, but at night."

Here, Mom has a spreading smile as this idea takes hold in her mind.

Joanna looks at her smile, still bewildered, when suddenly it hits her, "You want to strap the boys down in their beds at night, so they can't get out of bed?"

Something about this is still bothering Joanna, but then she suddenly remembers the boys unprotected heads hurtling towards certain injury or death, and she reconsiders. Mom sees Joanna's thought process on her face and is slowly nodding her head.

Joanna finally says, "OK, I'll get the straps and hide them in the boy's laundry before I give it back to you, so nobody will see that I gave them to you."

Dad walks up to the women, and asks much too loudly,

"Well, can we get the straps?"

Mom now says,

"Shhhhh, hush Honey. Joanna will do it, but she can get in trouble."

Mom looks around to make sure Buck was not overheard. She knows how his voice carries. Dad is unconcerned, just nods his head. Joanna hurries away, as Mom and Dad go back to help with the boys, and their eventual departure. Mom and Dad are tremendously pleased that they will soon get to take their kids home, and this whole nasty business will be behind them. Dad begins to sing one of his favorite songs from Perry Como, "You'll never walk alone."

"…at the end of the storm

Is a golden day

And the sweet silver song of a lark…"

Home, Deadly, Home

Time passes with the exquisite slowness enjoyed by the young and hated by the old. For the young, there is always time enough for everything, and days stretch out to what seems like weeks, prolonging the enjoyment of many delightful events. Over the next three months, summer and all the associated unpleasant memories are forgotten, and Thanksgiving approaches.

Mom stands over the kitchen sink, doing dishes, and as is often the case, her mind wanders to the past. She has this time to herself. Buck is in the Living Room watching TV, Eddie is taking a nap in his carrier five feet away, and Danny & Wayne are out playing. Ha! That's pretty funny; she almost said they were out *back* playing. That would imply she can control where they run. Telling them to stay in the back yard (or house for that matter) has never worked. Punishment doesn't work either. Sometimes Buck can put the "Fear of God" in them for an hour or two, but it never lasts. Mom thinks about her conversation with Buck last night about wanting to have "just one more child", which she hopes…prays…is a girl. Of course, Dad wants another Son; he often jokes about wanting five boys so he can have his own basketball team. Mom is not amused by this in the least. She miscarried her first child (which was a girl), then she was in labor for 58 hours with Danny because she went into labor a little early, and her doctor was out. Nobody else knew that she could not give birth naturally because of her narrow hips. She has endured a lot of pain for so little in return from her boys; so little joy, so much trouble. Just two boys have made her feel as if she has aged ten years. She pauses, turning just enough to look at her beautiful boy, Eddie, peacefully sleeping for once. He sure has a set of lungs on him. She and Buck had thought he had colic or some other medical condition that caused him to cry so much—the Doctor said no, that some babies just cried for no apparent reason. She glances up at the clock on the wall, and gets comfort that it is just after ten. If Eddie sleeps a little longer, and Danny and Wayne stay gone a while longer, she will have some more quiet time. It's just a question of when before Eddie becomes one of the boys, a member of the tribe. Then, there will be three boys running amok, instead of just two. It doesn't seem that long ago, that she gazed down on Danny, then Wayne in the same way, and they looked so innocent—so pure. For the thousandth time, she wonders what happened to her boys. She has always been tremendously loving and attentive to them. Buck has been too, in his own way. Mom thinks back to last year, when Buck and Danny were out on the front sidewalk. They had such fun. Oh, what fun they had…until.

Buck is out on the front sidewalk throwing Danny high into the air (she can't be sure, but she knows it is over ten feet, and probably much higher), and then catching him under his arms before he hits the sidewalk. On one of these particularly high throws, Buck misses Danny, and Danny hits his head on the sidewalk. Danny's head is bleeding, and he is screaming.

Buck says, "Now, look what you just did. You broke the sidewalk!"

Dad squats down beside him and points to a crack in the sidewalk that was already there (of course) for years, now covered with blood splatter. Mom walks over and picks Danny up into her arms, just as he stops crying, pondering the enormity of the crime he has just committed. Buck never apologizes to Danny; doesn't even give him a hug. He is immensely proud of himself, however, in coming up with the broken sidewalk bit, and loves to tell people the story.

Several months later, Buck is trying to help Mom, by getting Danny out of his high-chair. He reaches down, grabs Danny's right arm, and yanks up. The result is a full separation of the arm from the shoulder. Dad knows what happened because he feels and hears the bone give in his hand. Danny stands perfectly still in the seat of his high chair. His eyes are wide, staring off at nothing in particular, as the unimaginable pain starts to build. The scream starts at a low-level, and then rises to a volume like he and his parents never knew was possible. Mom tries to comfort him, while Dad stands off to the side dispassionately studying the situation.

Finally, Dad says, "I'll take him."

Dad swoops in and picks up Danny, taking enormous strides to the car. Mom knows he is taking Danny to the emergency room.

Since that day, she has never said anything to Buck about what happened because she knows he feels remorseful enough—in his own way. Mom thinks about the boys again. She and Buck try to create a structured environment for the boys; they make sure the boys kneel at their bunks and pray every night; and over each meal. They go to church, every Sunday, and she and Buck believe in the scripture, "Spare the rod, spoil the child"…Boy do they ever. Mom looks over at a sleeping Eddie, and decides she has time to run to the bathroom for a few minutes. She pats her hands dry with a towel, and then quietly slips around the corner.

Danny has been peeking through the kitchen window at his Mom, waiting for her to leave the kitchen. As soon as he sees her move into the hall, he slips into the kitchen, quickly pulls a chair over to the counter, climbs up on the chair, then the counter, and moves towards the refrigerator. Once he gets to the refrigerator, it is too high to scale, so he opens the cabinet next to it, then uses just the tips of his fingers and toes to scale to the top of the cabinet. Once there, however, Danny realizes the cabinet door is blocking him. Without hesitating, and without any clear fear of heights…or falling, Danny grabs a hold of the top of the cabinet door then pushes with his feet and swings the door over beside the refrigerator where he lets go with his left hand, which very adeptly reaches out and knocks the hangman's noose to the floor. He pushes back until he is just over the counter and drops down. He is careful to close the cabinet door. Danny then moves quickly to the chair, scrambles down, moves the chair back to the kitchenette, picks up the hangman's noose, and peeks around the corner to make sure Mom isn't coming, and then runs for the backyard where Wayne is playing. His entire trip takes less than two minutes. Danny was quiet enough that he never waked Eddie, and Mom never sees any indication Danny was ever here.

No more than a minute after Danny is safely in the backyard, Mom returns to the kitchen. She walks over to Eddie, tucks the blanket around him (whether it needs it or not), and then returns to the dishes. It isn't long before she is once again lost in her thoughts. She thinks back to just two weeks before her due date with Eddie, and shakes her head with the strong memory, and a small smile barely touches her lips at the absurdity of it all.

Mom is yawning as she leaves the hallway, and steps into the kitchen, to make breakfast for Buck and the boys. She places her right foot into the barely-lit kitchen, and immediately begins to slide. If she hadn't had her hand on the door jamb, she no doubt would have fallen and hurt herself, and probably her unborn child, Eddie. Before her on the floor, grease covered every inch of the kitchen. On top of the stove is the broiler pan (filled with hamburger grease), she left there the night before. The broiler pan grill was removed and is sitting on the nearby counter, and all the grease collected in the bottom was removed by tiny fingers and re-deposited on the floor. Covering the grease, some topping perhaps, is a random, scattered mix of corn, green beans, peas, carrots, and mixed vegetables. Over near the refrigerator, are the discarded cardboard containers, for these fine frozen, Birds-eye products. Mom was strangely at peace as she surveyed the destruction. Because of her calmness, she takes in more details, and notices that even the paper labels on the frozen vegetable boxes were ripped off. She moves to her left, and opens the freezer top to the refrigerator, and confirms her suspicions. Every single box of Birds-eye vegetables that are remaining (15 or more is her estimate) has its label removed. There is not a single label in the freezer, but a quick scan of the kitchen finds a neat stack on the counter right next to the refrigerator. Mom realizes that without the labels to identify what's inside, for the next few weeks, it will be a surprise as to what vegetable they will have each night for dinner. Mom thinks that each time the boys do something like this it will be the last time. At the very least, it couldn't get any worse...Boy, is she wrong about that! What bothers her most is that what she sees is almost chaos. She thinks she can accept it better if it is 100 percent chaos. At least then she can pretend that the boy's actions are a force of nature; a tornado, a hurricane maybe...some random event. Instead, by seeing the neatly stacked broiler, and the neatly stacked vegetable cartons, and labels, she realizes, there is intelligence behind this. This revelation bothers her on the same level as discovering a tornado is a sentient being and can lay out its own path of destruction.

Mom comes back to the present again with an effort...too much pain in the past. Danny, he's the key. She despises herself for always coming back to him, but she knows he is at the center of everything bad that has ever happened. Buck thinks she always over-reacts, or sees things that aren't there, but he isn't here all day with them as she is. It's that look Danny gives her, when she gets within listening distance of him and Wayne. When Danny and Wayne have their heads together, and Danny is whispering in that weird, fast way he has, she will get the look.

Danny's look says, "I was about to impart the secrets of the universe to my young apprentice here, but now you have ruined it."

Once, while dusting the furniture she caught the tail-end of something Danny was telling Wayne,

"...I will throw you in the ocean. Then a big fish will eat you all up. Then I will go out and catch that fish, and then have Mommy cook it up, so when I eat it, I will be eating you! See what will happen if you don't do what I say?"

I had no idea what it was that Danny wanted Wayne to do, but I'm sure it wasn't good...it never is.

Danny and Wayne sit at the picnic table. We, the constant witnesses, are once again standing near the boys. We are never certain what we are about to witness, but we know we are here for a reason. I happened to be admiring the beautiful watermelon colored flowers on a Crape Myrtle, and had just turned towards the walnut tree, noticing for the first time the wooden steps nailed to the trunk, which lead up to a platform above, when a sudden movement from Danny catches my attention.

I think, "Here we go again."

As I move in closer, I see that Danny has stood up and is removing something hidden under his shirt. Danny lays it down on the table in front of him.

Wayne says, "Ohhhh, you aren't supposed to have that. Daddy said no!"

It isn't terribly often that Wayne speaks up against Danny, and as we look closer we see why. Lying in front of Danny is a hangman's noose.

The night before, Dad had a piece of rope which was long enough, and since he knew how, he decided to make the noose. Where he learned this skill he didn't remember, but we have no doubt that this is the real deal. After he made it, then demonstrated on the back of a chair how easily it tightened, but how it was almost impossible to loosen back up, he put it on top of the refrigerator, out of reach (or so he thought.) Mom argued for the dismantling of this killing device immediately because the kids might get a hold of it. It was no use. Dad laughed at Mom calling her a 'Nervous Nelly' that it would be fine.

Now Danny is playing with the hangman's noose by grasping the tight knot with one hand and the longer rope with the other, then pulling on the longer rope, watching the noose get smaller. He takes hold of the knot and pulls on the noose until it gets bigger. Danny may not know this, but he is performing this action exactly as his Dad did the night before. He has an uncanny ability at mimicry. He is totally lost in thought as he continues performing this tighten-loosen-tighten-loosen activity over and over with the single-mindedness of an "Idiot-Savant."

Across the table, Wayne watches Danny uneasily. We are on guard as well, even though Danny's intentions seem to be benign.

Mom wonders what Danny and Wayne are up to and is a little worried by how quiet they are. Another memory comes to her of a long time ago, when Danny was just two, or thereabouts. She and Buck saw him totally different back then. He seemed to be sensitive and normal then. He had discovered a sugar ant on the back of the sink, and was playing with it by putting his finger down to make it turn around, then moving his finger back in front of it. Evidently, he had played this game for a while; he never tired, and either did the ant. The game ended suddenly when Danny accidentally put his finger down on the ant, and it quit moving. He was so distraught over that, he acted as if he had lost a pet dog, or a family member. How can she reconcile the Danny from then with the one of today? She and Buck have had many discussions about Danny, trying to figure him out. At times, because of his cruel and violent nature, they think that maybe he is missing some critical part of brain material, or functionality. Maybe his destiny is to have low intelligence. Maybe he will be a criminal, no matter how they raise him. They know he is smart. They have known this since Danny was five months old, and was in his carrier in the backseat of their car. Mom had his bottle.

She and Buck have been trying to get Danny to talk for a long time now, but both know they are still a long way off before it happens. Mom takes a water bottle from Danny, and as was the custom, is now going to hand him a juice bottle. She holds the juice bottle below the seat, as she turns to look at Danny.

She says, "What do I have in my hand? What do I have?"

Dad interrupts with, "Why are you wasting your time with that? You know he hasn't even tried to say anything."

Dad laughs and shakes his head at the absurdity of what she is doing.

Mom tries again, "What do I have in my hand? If you tell me, you can have it."

Dad said, "I told y ..."

"The bottle," is said in a small but clear voice from the backseat, which causes Mom and Dad to turn towards Danny, who is sitting peacefully with his hand outstretched, waiting for the bottle. Mom and Dad turn to look at each other in amazement.

Dad says, "What the heck was that? Did I just hear him say what I think he said?"

Mom responds, "Yes, what else could it have been?"

They spent the remainder of the day and much of the following week trying to get Danny to say anything else at all, but no luck. In fact, it was quite a few months before he said another word.

She comes back to the present and sighs heavily.

She says, "Heaven help me!"

Mom is thankful for many things, and Buck finally finishing college is one of them. Three years of 8 AM to 2 PM classes, then off to clerking at the Post Office until midnight, then home again and studying until early morning, then starting all over again, was tiring on everyone. Sure he came home for lunch and between classes, but that time was all for studying; very little time for the wife and kids. The kids hardly ever saw their Dad at all. When Dad was home, he was usually studying, so none of the kids better ever disturb him! Now he is working days from 7am to 4pm, and home at nights.

Mom thinks about how the hospital straps have been a Godsend. Each night, Danny & Wayne get under the covers of their beds. Buck flips up the covers and sheets at their feet and attaches the straps on each side to an ankle. Buck had previously attached the other ends of the straps to the frame, and let the weight of the mattresses help hold them in place. She knows they have passed the escape test, because after the first night of strapping the boys down, and turning the hall light out, she and Buck crept back to the partly open door and watched what would happen. As they suspected, Danny rose up on one elbow as he stared at the door. Beneath his covers, we could see that his legs were alternately doing jumping jacks and bicycle kicks...testing the straps. Suddenly Danny disappeared under the covers, we could see that he was totally folded in half, and his hands were feverishly testing the straps around each ankle. This activity went on for a surprisingly long time. I had to admire him for his persistence. Then, we saw his hand sneak out from under the covers on the side of his bed facing us, tracing the strap down to the frame then feeling where the strap passes between the mattress and frame, and getting very still as in deep thought. Every time he tried to rock into a new position, to try to get free, the other strap stopped him. One last desperate move was finally tried, which surprised us in its quiet and crazy nature. Danny moved back and centered himself in a splits maneuver at the foot of his mattress, grabbed the footboard with both hands, and flung himself over the edge. I remember letting out a gasp and started to go through the door, but Buck pulled me back. Buck was utterly fascinated watching Danny. As I watched him, I see that I needn't have worried. His hands easily extended out and stopped his body (and face) from hitting the floor. He balanced on his hands as his feet are still securely fastened above. He twisted and kicked, and studied his predicament. We saw he wasn't going to harm himself, so watched intently, his next actions. It was as if we were watching a young Houdini practice his craft. Danny soon understood what we had already realized; the straps that were over the footboard had locked in place, meaning he couldn't get either side to slide off of the footboard and down to the side, where he may be able to get it loose. He became very still after realizing he was at an impasse, so walked on his hands backward, then (easier than we might have imagined possible) climbed backwards up the footboard, neatly ducking under the covers, then a moment later his head poked back out of the top. A sound from Danny is never heard; not even any sound of frustration. How odd that boy is. She remembers that right after Danny got settled, a small voice broke the silence.

Wayne suddenly whispered, "You almost did it," Wayne said, with real admiration in his voice.

This startled us because we hadn't realized Wayne was awake and watching him. He was waiting patiently for Danny to escape then help him escape too. Mom is still convinced, as is Dad that without Danny's negative influence Wayne would be a great kid. To the best of their knowledge, Danny never tried to escape the straps again.

We continue to watch Danny uneasily as he plays with the noose, and remember we have a history with Danny, and do not trust him. As soon as we have this thought, without any warning, whatsoever, Danny throws the noose over Wayne's head until it is around his neck, then he pulls tight. Wayne is surprised just as suddenly as we are. He doesn't even have a chance to make a sound of distress. Wayne's eyes immediately grow wide and bulge out as the rope continues to tighten. Danny is not saying a word but is pulling with all his might. He has the focus of someone who takes his job seriously; in fact, as Danny stands, then steps up on the seat, and begins to lean back, he resembles a fisherman strapped to the seat in the back of a fishing boat, fighting to land a prize marlin. Wayne, knowing he is in real trouble this time—that he can't breathe and that he doesn't have much time—stands up, grabs hold of the rope in front of him, then begins to pull with everything he has. Danny accepts the challenge and re-doubles his efforts. He is gritting his teeth now, and once again the evil smile resurfaces on his face. The more Wayne struggles, the more Danny is enjoying this. He knows this is a one-way trip. Dad said last night that it will tighten, but will not loosen. Danny is counting on this fact. His reverie is interrupted by a sudden loosening of the rope, which causes him to fall backwards on his butt. Wayne, in an act of desperation, decides to drive forward, to try to knock Danny off-balance, and maybe Danny will drop the rope, and he can get free. If only he can get in the house, Mommy or Daddy can save him. Danny was surprised by this sudden loosening of the rope, but he is a game adversary, and grabs tighter to the rope, just as Wayne gets to his feet beside the table then starts running towards the back door. Wayne is pulling with his last lungful of precious air. It has only been ten seconds since his last breath (again, these things are happening much too fast) but, with almost super human strength Wayne moves step by step towards the back door, with Danny being dragged behind, holding on for dear life. Wayne's hands are digging desperately at the rope which is pulling tighter and now digging deeper into the skin around his neck. Danny, true to his species (that of a monster), hangs on for dear life, with no intention of letting go, no matter what happens. Like Captain Ahab, Danny is on a personal quest which only he understands; so damn the consequences. He will not give up. It is only twenty feet to the back door, but for Wayne, it seems like the length of the Mojave Desert. For Danny, dragging behind is fun; until he hits the three cement steps which lead up to the back porch. This is intensely painful, but Danny is resolute in his plan, and hangs on as first his elbows hit, then his knees. Wayne stops at the back door, and fumbles with the knob, giving Danny the chance to try to stand up. Just as he starts to get his feet under him, the back screen-door opens, and he falls back on his stomach as they are again traveling through the door and the laundry room then past the entrance to the Kitchen. Wayne sees his Mom standing in front of the sink and stops. Funny little white spots are running all over in front of everything he looks at, and even his Mom has spots on her.

Mom's thoughts are suddenly interrupted by the banging of the back door (very common), followed by the strangest sound she has ever heard…maybe a scream from a mute person, someone without vocal cords? She turns towards the sound and is momentarily paralyzed; Wayne is standing there with the hangman's noose Buck made last night pulled exceptionally tight around his neck. He is making horrible choking sounds, which explains what she heard. This doesn't make sense. The noose is on top of the refrigerator! She knows she isn't thinking clearly, so when she sees Danny still holding tightly to the rope, and still maintaining pressure, her anger drives her into motion. She strides forward quickly, first knocking Danny away from the rope, "Move!"

She then begins to work on loosening the noose from Wayne's neck while she starts yelling for Buck in the other room,

"Buck! Buck! Please Help Me!"

She can't get her fingers between Wayne's neck and the rope. How long has Wayne been without air?

"Please God, help me get this off," she cries.

Wayne is slowly dying. The color of the skin on his face is now dark red, and moving towards purple-blue. His eyes continue to bulge, but now they are glassy and unfocused, as well. He suddenly bends over and drops to one of his hands, head down, as Mom is still frantically digging for any hold she can. Time is short for Wayne, and they both know it. We glance at Danny and realize he has stood off to the side, as still as can be, with that strange stoic look, and his head slightly cocked to one side. We briefly wonder what Danny will do when Wayne finally dies. Will he smile? Will he celebrate in some way? Danny is making us have evil thoughts, and we refuse to let his deeds and thoughts affect us. We turn our attention back to Mom and Wayne, and suddenly Dad appears in the doorway at a run, and gets such a look of instant shock, it would be comical if in any other situation.

Mom says, "My Baby! Help me please!"

She hands Wayne's now still body over to Buck as she is saying it. Dad responds in the only way he knows as Mom was responding... without hesitation, without emotion. He quickly cradles his son in his arms in a tight embrace. Then using his extra strength, and knowledge of how the hangman's noose works, he has the damned thing off within seconds. Mom had reached the point in her efforts where she knew that Wayne was likely to die in her arms, and was saying silent prayers to God, beseeching Him to take her Baby to everlasting paradise. Wayne sucks in his first air in more than three minutes. Mom yells out with laughter as she sees Wayne coming back from the brink of death, and starts to hug him tight.

Dad warns her, "Hold on Hon, let him breathe. He's OK now."

Dad surprises us with this new persona by saying this so gently, with so much love, which is so different from the Dad we first met at the hospital. He hands Wayne over to Mom who continues to sit on the kitchen floor and now pulls him close and begins to rock him gently. Mom, now slowly tells Dad about what she saw. She admits, whatever happened outside is unknown, and she doesn't have a clue how Danny got the rope in the first place, but she fills Dad in on what she did see. Dad, unlike his usual self, is remarkably quiet and stone-faced. Mom's initial panic is starting to subside, and her heart-rate and breathing is slowing. She turns and stares at the noose lying on the floor.

She says, "That damned hangman's noose! I told you to get rid of that thing! I told you."

Dad looks down and nods his head. Again we are surprised by this new demeanor. We can hear Mom humming softly as she smiles down at Wayne, and sees his more-normal looking face looking back at her. Dad slowly stands and picks up the hangman's noose, goes to a drawer next to the sink, and retrieves a pair of scissors. With the practiced method of a person on an assembly line, Dad begins to cut the hangman's noose, and after several minutes, he has roughly 20 two-inch pieces of rope. He mumbles to himself as he finishes, and we barely hear him.

Dad is saying, "Let's see if he can do any harm with that. Let's just see."

Dad makes no attempt to clean-up the pieces of rope, but moves extremely quickly for Danny, grabs him by the shoulders (not particularly gently), then steers him towards the back bedrooms.

Mom yells to Dad, "Don't you dare lose your temper! I want to kill him too, but you better not!"

Mom continues to rock Wayne, asking him,

"Are you feeling better?" and "How are you now?" or "Would you like something to drink?"

Wayne answers all the questions right, so maybe he's going to be OK after all. Mom is so focused on Wayne; she barely acknowledges the shrill screams coming from the back part of the house, or the insistent screams coming from five feet away in the carrier. Mom continues, to slowly rock, back and forth, while she hums that song she likes so much by Roy Orbison, "Crying" as she smiles down at her precious baby. Mom's humming soon stops, as she rocks and cries; rocks and cries.

Green Valley

This is a Saturday in May of 1962. There have been six months of relative peace in the household, and for the first time in a very long time, Mom and Dad are starting to have real hope that their kids are on the road to being normal. Danny will be four in three months, Wayne is now three months past two, and Eddie is nine months. Danny is still a very serious child, and has a tendency to give you "The look" (A look of pure hatred. The, "I'm-going-to-kill-you" look), which angers she and Buck more than anything else he does. Wayne, who is just over a year behind Danny in age, is just a few inches shorter than he is. His fast growth seems to have adversely affected his coordination, since he trips and falls, and stumbles, and runs into everything. Dad has started calling Wayne, "An accident looking for a place to happen", or "Moose". Eddie has an interesting quirk of his own. Whenever he doesn't get his way, he will always throw a tantrum. Once, Mom was sitting at the desk writing checks, and her pen accidentally rolled off of the desk. Eddie was playing at Mom's feet, and was struck on the thigh by the falling pen… Instead of being merely startled like most children his age, he threw a tantrum. Recently, he has added holding his breath to the end of every tantrum. He will hold his breath—his face turning scarlet—until he passes out. Mom has asked the family doctor about this, and he advised her to not worry, because after passing out, Eddie always starts to breathe again. Mom has never heard of a child doing the passing out thing, and wonders when he will outgrow it. The doctor seems to think pretty soon. It's just another thing to worry about with the kids.

    The family has just left by the front door of their house and is on one of their many walks. Mom walks together with Danny and Wayne in front, while Dad follows up with the stroller carrying a sleeping Eddie. They have gone just a few dozen feet when they cross to the other side of the street. Their destination is a sidewalk which runs in front of a large parking lot. On the other side of this parking lot is a cluster of large buildings which make up San Gabriel Valley College; the college Dad attended for three years for his degree in electronics. We, the faithful witnesses, trail behind the family, enjoying this beautiful sunny day. We can see and hear dozens of sprinklers scattered all around the campus (wherever there is green), adding their "ch-ch-ch" voices to the sound of cars in the distance, and a low-flying single-engine airplane above. As is the case on most days, the air pollution creates a light fog, blanketing everything, even on the sunniest of days. Mom and Dad are walking slowly, and taking the time to stop and look at anything that catches anyone's attention. The first place they stop is at a red and yellow number "57", painted on the sidewalk. From this number is a black arrow pointing towards a huge pine tree. This tree has no more business being here than some huge boulder in a Midwest farmer's field left over from the retreat of the previous glacier. First of all, it is the only pine tree within sight (Mom and Dad spin in a circle to verify this, as do we.) Second, all the other trees scattered about the campus are Palms, Elms, Pepper, and Eucalyptus trees. Mom and Dad wonder how they have never *really looked* at this tree before, given its size. Danny is very excited as he says,

    "I know what this is! It's an arrow marking out a pirate's treasure!"

    It doesn't matter to Danny that they live far from the ocean, where a pirate's booty would be more likely to be found. Danny and Wayne run to the tree, several yards away, and disappear under its massive boughs. Mom and Dad wait patiently. Who are they to interfere in a search for pirate's treasure? The search is thorough and fast, as both boys come back a little disappointed. This disappointment only lasts until the next adventure is discovered.

At the end of the block, they come to a cross street (Grant), but they have already moved off the sidewalk towards an area at the southeast corner of the intersection, which is on the property of the college. Danny and Wayne are now bouncing with almost unrestrained excitement.

They yell in unison, "Green Valley! Green Valley! Can we go in?"

They have locked eyes with their Dad, who has a huge grin as he says,

"Go ahead!"

The boys soon disappear into a huge hedge, by one of the many trails. If you were to look down at this panorama from above, you would see it as a single hedge (in reality, it is a series of smaller bushes grown together), stretching fifty yards in each direction, with dozens of trails winding round and round with no rhyme or reason to their design. Some trails cross over other trails many times, some just run into dead ends. The magic of this place comes from the disregard for normal rules; the trails aren't straight, and there is no logic to where they go in, or come out. In the boy's minds, they enter the trails in this world, and come out in another world; where boys sail ships, swim in lagoons with mermaids, or maybe get to see real dinosaurs. Anything is possible in "Green Valley" (named by Danny long ago, for whatever reasons he had then…but now long forgotten). When running the trails, the boys are lost in time and space. They feel the exhilaration of non-stop running, with the twisting and turning down new and random trails, tripping over exposed roots often, but having the balance of the young, hardly ever notice—or fall down. Each time they take a trail, they just know this is the new one they have never taken before that will take them to the magic places. The boys sometimes pass, and occasionally almost run into each other. There is no anger when they do so…the boys hardly notice each other…they are lost to their imaginations (with looks of total happiness on their faces) as they hope their transportations will soon happen. All too soon both of the boys hear a train whistle intruding on their fantasies. They try to ignore this sound, but it is insistent and they know what it is, and if they don't soon obey this whistle they will get into trouble. Both boys leave their fantasies and start to run towards the sound of the train, taking twist after twist until they emerge from the hedge within a few feet of their parents. Dad is just lowering (and un-cupping) his hands from his face where he had produced a really good train whistle sound.

They continue on their journey across the parking lot to Grant Street. Coming out on the sidewalk at Grant, the two boys look nervously south across the street. This is the part of the walk they dread, since they have to walk past the "Witches House." Like the huge pine tree they saw earlier, this house is out-of-place and does not belong here among the Spanish and Ranch style, single-story homes of the area. Mom and Dad have hardly noticed this house until they start paying attention to the reactions and whispered conversations between Danny and Wayne. This house is a huge two-story with used-to-be-white paint, which has turned grey (black wood shows where the paint has already flaked off.) The house has dormer windows (with off-white curtains which are never fully closed) all around the roof line, crenulated towers, spires, and old-fashioned exaggerated style lightning rods encircling the entire roof. These have *fleur-de-lis* patterns which climb up to the business end of the rods...wickedly sharp points. Mom and Dad glance for a few seconds, and make comments like, "That is such an odd place", or "It must be very old", before completely erasing it from their minds. To the boys, they are drawn by a force which seems to emanate from this house, and every time they walk by here, they swear they can see a monster or a Witch peeking through the curtains behind some of the dormer windows. Another troubling thing an observer notices is that all around the house, there is no grass. It would be impossible to tell if there ever was. It appears that the desert, which once spread throughout this county, has reclaimed just this property. It is as if this was an empty lot, then one day the house just mysteriously materialized here. To further prove this point, we see no living bushes or trees on this property at all. Two trees, and three bushes, which have all died some time ago, can no longer be identified as to what they used to be. Most of the branches on trees and bushes alike have either broken off or been trimmed. If you would think this place has all the clues of an abandoned house, you would be wrong. At the back of the property, they can barely make out the top of a stairway, which leads down a hidden hillside at the back of this property. The only reason the boys know the cliff and stairs are there, is because they have looked back this way while walking across the bridge on Mt. Vernon, while on one of their Saturday family walks. The bridge crosses over a cement spillway, used for flood control, which has a barbed wire fence running down both sides. The bottom of the stairs is three feet from the barbed wire fence. As hard as they have tried, neither Danny nor Wayne has seen any hole in the fence, or any way down to the bottom of the spillway. The only thing that makes sense to them is that there is a secret boat in the spillway, or there is a secret cave they can only see once they get to the bottom. Otherwise, why are the steps there? Parked at the end of a gravel driveway at the back of the house is a black 1959 Mercedes-Benz Sedan, which is way too shiny for this place. We would feel better if an old, rusted out, and missing tire, clunker were parked there instead. Of course, the sedan adds to the vampire story the boys have created, but does little for the witch or monster. The boys decide that a vampire, a witch, and a monster all live there together. This story works in their minds, and that's OK. This house is way too close to home, and these boys feel this threat in parts of their psyche they don't yet understand. Regardless of any misgivings, they are excited by this place too. Imagine if a real witch, or monster, or maybe Dracula himself lived in the house? Danny makes a mental note to return here later with Wayne, so they can explore the house more thoroughly. Both boys come out of their thoughts at the same time and realize Mom and Dad have started on without them. They hurry to catch up, eager to get to their next destination; the Circle K on Mt. Vernon, where everyone gets ice cream. Mom is now skipping ahead while holding Wayne and Eddie's hands. A 1962 canary yellow Pontiac Grand Prix cruises by. All of the windows are down, and Sheb Wooley is belting out, "Purple People Eater".

    Danny slows down to walk with his Dad as he stares after the yellow car in the distance. Danny does not believe in coincidence. To him, everything happens for a reason, and he spends much of his time pondering why things are happening at certain times. Now, he is in deep thought about why a yellow car would be playing a song about a purple monster that eats people. A part of his mind makes the connection with the monsters in the Witches House. He just has to figure out the significance of the colors. As quickly as Danny went into deep thought, he comes out of it. He has plenty of time to think on this mystery and others that are currently clogging his mind. He looks up at his Dad beside him and smiles. His Dad smiles back as only he can, and puts his arm around Danny's shoulder.

He says, "You doing alright Danny?"

Danny says, "Yes Daddy. I think I'll get strawberry ice cream today."

"You always get strawberry ice cream!" Dad says with a fake punch to Danny's arm and a big smile.

Without thinking about it (aren't most actions with children spontaneous though?), Danny starts to sing one of their favorite songs, and it never occurs to him the irony of choosing to sing "The Witch Doctor, " by Alvin and the Chipmunks,

"…And then the Witch Doctor, he told me what to do

He said to …

Ooo, eee, ooo, ah, ah, ting, tang, walla, walla, bing, bang…"

The Big Lie

It is June of 1962, again on a Saturday, and Danny and Wayne have been watching Tom and Jerry. They both like this cartoon because Wayne says he is Jerry, and Danny gets to be Tom. We have been sitting with them, and things are relaxed; no noise and no fighting for once, which is a blessing to Mom and Dad, now sitting in the dining room. Inga, a Chihuahua (the new addition to the family given to them from their Mom's female friend Joe), lies on the couch between Danny and Wayne. Inga is not asleep because the boys frighten her with their sudden outbursts too often. She is getting petted by Danny and Wayne, but she is ready to flee to the safety of Mom and Dad in a moment, when things change. As the show ends, Danny hops up and tells Wayne it's time to go outside and play. We have noticed that as Wayne gets older he is resisting Danny more often, and he does so this time by saying he doesn't feel like going out, but wants to stay and watch more TV. Danny stands and stares at Wayne for a half a minute with that same blank look we have gotten used to seeing. Wayne does his part by not looking at Danny; pretending like he isn't even there. Without saying another word, Danny spins on his heels and walks quickly out of the house and into the back yard. Once he gets there he stops in front of the garage and kicks at little rocks at his feet. He is in deep thought, and appears to have no destination in mind, so we relax. Danny becomes extremely still and turns his head towards the fence that separates their yard from their next door neighbor's (Bucky Sánchez). Danny thinks back to last year and the trouble he had with Bucky. The trouble both he *and* Wayne had.

Bucky Sánchez plays with Danny & Wayne often, is about a year older than Danny, and has five older brothers and sisters. Bucky and his family are the ones who taught Danny and Wayne Spanish over the past few years, which is an admirable thing, but also a terrible thing; They also pick up every dirty word and phrase from Bucky. They both consider this part a bonus, since they know words their Mom doesn't know; they can get away with saying whatever they want. What a delightful feeling of empowerment this is...for the first few days at least. Mom notices that Danny and Wayne speak Spanish often with Bucky whenever he is over. She also notices that some words are more enjoyable to speak for the boys, than others. They always grin like Cheshire Cats, and Bucky will always shake his head and give them a look like, "Don't say that now!" Mom's curiosity is sufficiently piqued, so she makes a trip over to see Bucky's Mom, Rosita, for an explanation. Rosita sits Bucky down on the sofa and Mom sits Danny and Wayne down next to him. Danny and Wayne will not break, but Bucky does. After all, he was the one who supplied the distinctive vocabulary to Danny and Wayne.

Danny blinks several times as he comes back to the present. He decides to head over to Bucky's. Yes, his plan will work perfectly there. When he starts moving he is doing so slowly with his head down, his shoulders slumped, and his feet shuffling. It is puzzling to us why Wayne not playing with him has him so down, since he has never been bothered by that in the past. In fact, Danny has always done well by himself. We follow him as he goes out through the back gate, into the alley, a turn left, then goes over to the Sánchez's gate, and without hesitating, walks into their back yard. The Sánchez house is hot-pink stucco, with white trim. They have a single orange tree and single apple tree in each corner of the yard, that provide fruit which is not quite as appetizing like what can be bought at the store. There are no flowers or bushes, and at the back of the house is a covered patio. Danny has spent many an hour playing under this cover with Bucky while it is raining. With six kids under the age of 16, there is always someone on the patio, and this is no exception. Bucky's older sister, Carmen, sits on a patio chair with her feet up on the table, painting her toenails. She has on white shorts, and a white blouse, a simple pair of gold earrings, her brown hair pulled back in a pony tail, her brown eyes have no makeup, but there is a hint of lipstick on her lips (after all, she is only 13, and this concession from her Mom on the lipstick was "huge"). She sees Danny walking towards the house across the back yard.

She says, "Hola, Miguel. ¿Cómo estás?"

She then turns and yells through the partially open door, "Bucky! Miguel is here!"

Danny doesn't go through the door like he always does, but sits down in an empty lawn chair, and lowers his head. Usually Carmen doesn't pay attention to little kids, but this one she likes. She stops painting her toenails and looks at Danny.

She asks, "What's the matter with you? Are you sick?"

Danny shakes his head and doesn't respond. Carmen stands up and walks to the sliding door, pulls the screen aside, then leans her head into the house.

She yells, "Mama, ¿dónde estás?"

There are a few moments of silence, then Mrs. Sánchez (Rosita) meets Carmen in the doorway, then Carmen whispers something, as she turns and points to Danny. Carmen stands aside as Rosita walks out onto the porch, then she goes in and closes the door. Bucky can be seen in the living room beyond the glass speaking to Carmen, and then he goes over and sits on the couch. If his Mom closed the door, it was so she could be alone. Rosita walks out onto the porch with her eyes locked on the lowered head of Danny and sits down next to him, taking his hand.

EDEN FADING

She asks him, "¿Qué pasa, mi hijo?"

Danny just shakes his head. We have moved in close because what we see in Danny's behavior is so new to us. Rosita switches to English.

She says, "Danny, what is wrong? Please tell me."

In a very soft voice, we have never heard him use before, Danny says, "My brother Wayne died."

We are just as astonished as Rosita. Danny is so convincing, for a moment; we believe him too. Then we remember we just left Wayne in front of the TV at home, and begin to wonder what game Danny is playing.

Rosita says, "What was that you just said? Tell me again."

"My brother Wayne died"

Rosita leans closer so she can look directly into Danny's eyes and sees such sadness there, her heart breaks.

She begins to ask more probing questions, "What happened?"

"He stepped on a nail"

"When did it happen?"

"Yesterday, he stepped on the nail, and he got sick and went to the hospital, and his foot swelled up, and he died."

"Where are your parents?"

"In my house, talking to the cemetery people"

She stares at him, thinking about his answers. It doesn't sound right to her, but she is talking to a four-year old, and he is probably majorly confused with all the details of what has happened. Rosita's husband, Sergio walks out on the porch, sliding the door closed behind him.

He says, "Hola Miguel."

He doesn't finish, but sits down across from Rosita and Danny, saying,

"What has happened?"

"Danny just told me that his brother Wayne died yesterday," Rosita says.

Sergio responds with soft and compassionate sympathy, "What?"

With six children of his own, and these Walker boys almost like his own, he feels a genuine loss. He wipes his eyes after a few moments, and then looks up at Danny.

He asks, "What happened to Wayne, Miguel?"

"He stepped on a nail"

"When did he step on the nail?"

"Yesterday, he stepped on the nail, and he got sick and went to the hospital, and his foot swelled up, and he died."

"Where was the nail?"

"My Daddy forgot it in our back yard after he built the shelves."

"Who is at your house now?"

"Just my Mommy and Daddy are there. They are talking to the cemetery people."

Sergio and Rosita escort Danny into the house where Bucky's aunt and uncle are visiting, and who also know the Walker boys well. Each of them take turns grilling Danny on what happened, and he answers them the same way every time. His story never changes. Even though they all comment to each other that there is something strange about the story, in the end, they are thoroughly convinced that Wayne is indeed dead. We, the witnesses, have been both, spellbound, and disturbed by what we have witnessed. Rosita sends Danny home to comfort his grieving parents. Danny walks out of the back gate at the same slow walk, with his head down. As soon as he has turned the corner in the alley, he begins to run, goes through his own gate and across his yard, then into his house. Once he is safely in the house, he stops in the laundry room, and the most evil, smug smile we have ever seen, appears on his face. Danny is positively giddy with excitement, and we can hear a very low laugh coming from him while he bounces up and down. He has just given the performance of his life. He was able to make up a story and convince four adults he was telling the truth. In his young mind, somehow he is getting even with Wayne for not playing with him, by convincing the neighbors he is dead. The ringing of the front doorbell interrupts Danny's "party for one", and the incessant barking of Inga. Danny walks over to the hallway wall, and peers around the corner so he can see the front door, as his Mom opens it. Mr. and Mrs. Sánchez are standing there on the porch with hands folded in front of them, with the aunt and uncle standing behind them. Out on the street a black 1962 Buick Electra 225 Convertible goes by and "I'm sorry," by Brenda Lee is playing from the radio.

Sergio says, "We just heard from Danny that Wayne died yesterday. We have come here to express our condolences."

Mom, confused like one would expect, says, "Excuse me?"

"We are here to pay our respects to your son Wayne," Sergio continues.

Mom stands motionless for a few seconds as her mind tries to wrap around what she has just heard. She finally turns toward the family room.

She yells, "Wayne, come here please."

Now it's the Sánchez's turn to look shocked, and more shocked yet, when Wayne walks up and stops next to his Mom…not dead. Mom finally seizes on what Mr. Sánchez first said, "We just heard from Danny…" Mom spins quickly and sees Danny before he has a chance to escape.

She says, "Freeze Mister! You go to your bedroom now, and don't you dare move!"

She turns back to the Sánchez's not sure what she can say to make things right.

She finally says, "I apologize for my Son. I think we can straighten this out in just a few minutes. Please come in."

She lets them in and leads them to the sofa and chairs in the family room, and sure enough; it takes just a few minutes to settle it all out. She apologizes again because she feels she can't apologize enough for what Danny has done. She plans on making him go over and apologize later, but not this soon after what he just did. They all stand up, and she tells them she will ask them over for dinner sometime soon. She stands on the porch stoop watching them walk slowly back home. They weren't entirely happy when they left, and she isn't sure the relationship between the two families will ever be the same after this, but she has done all she can for now. She is so angry now…and embarrassed. Despite her little voice telling her to wait for Buck to get home, so he can dole out the punishment, she decides it can't wait. She goes to her bedroom first and grabs one of Buck's belts from his side of the closet. She then goes back to the boy's bedroom where Danny sits on the lower bed of a bunk bed, with Wayne right beside him. As soon as Wayne sees the belt, he runs for the door and disappears. We have seen Danny at his worst, then as a normal child, and now bad again. We have no interest in seeing him punished. We step out into the hallway just before Mom closes the door. We have taken only a few steps when we hear the first "thwaaack…" then the cry of pain that follows. We realize that this cry has a quality of outrage to it. The audacity of his Mom in punishing him upsets him beyond the pain itself. We wish this piece of information will provide a clue which will bring us a little closer to understanding Danny, but understanding eludes us. We can hear a song coming from the radio in the kitchen, which is creating a strange *new* song with the "thwaaack…yell" back beat from the bedroom. The song is from Elvis Presley, "The Devil in Disguise."

Day of Sacrifice

It is now August of 1962, and we are traveling with the family in their royal blue 1956 Mercury, from their home in San Bernardino to Elsinore; about a 45 minute drive. It is now just after six o'clock in the evening since the family didn't leave until after Dad got home from work, and they were able to eat a quick dinner. Elsinore is the place of Mom's roots; she was born there, grew up there, and graduated high school there. While Mom was in high school, she first met Dad, who was a friend of her brother. Dad moved from Indiana to Elsinore, to live with his older sister. He soon met Mom, and the rest happened to bring us here to this moment, with Mom and Dad in the front seat, and their three children in the back. The family makes this trip every other weekend, leaving on Friday night, and returning late Sunday evening. The car is now past Paris, so there will be "twisty" roads (as the boys call them) for the next fifteen minutes. Much of this trip happens over desolate landscape with large rocks and boulders scattered as far as the horizon, and the occasional cactus. The highlight of the trip is when they come upon a large Indian arrow, stuck in the desert sand at a 45° angle just off the road. The arrow is thirty feet long, and a couple feet in diameter (and is actually a buried telephone pole), with feathers included. The boys always stare in awe at the remnant of the giant

Indian who fired that arrow, and secretly hope he never comes back to retrieve the arrow while they are in the area. It is fifteen minutes later and all three boys come awake with the sound of the tires leaving the pavement and entering a loud gravel road, with the associated swerving of the car, and the pungent smell of dust that fights its way into the car. There is the roller-coaster feeling when they first drop down a hill, then rapidly rise to the top of the next one, then immediately fall again (made more realistic by Dad's fondness for speed). After the next hill is crested, Lake Elsinore comes into view, with all the houses huddled up against its waters, and the Ortega Mountains on the other side of the lake, looming over all like a protective giant. Danny and Wayne are now leaning forward on the edge of their seats with excitement, borne of expectation of the weekend to come. Their excitement comes from their grandparents living here, but so do many aunts, uncles, and cousins. They are tremendously excited about all the adventures they will have this weekend. This includes the vast expanse of desert and hills; which they think is theirs to do as they please (there is never anyone else except their family, no matter where they go). The boys feel like many explorers who tamed native land before back through history, who have become enchanted by being the first person who has ever set eyes on a new river, or mountain range, or ocean. They can't wait until they finish breakfast tomorrow morning and get to head out. They wonder what Dad will have in mind, and savor the incredible feeling of unknown surprises. We have just turned right at the end of the gravel road, on to a paved road again, then after a few moments, pull over to park in front of a modest home, surrounded by a three-foot high stone wall. There is an Iron Gate set in the center of the wall, and two palm trees standing sentry duty at each corner of the lawn. Danny and Wayne exit the car and stand at the side of the car waiting for their Mom and Dad (Mom is now retrieving Eddie). They both stand there and breathe deeply. They love the strong smell of sage brush, which seems to penetrate and stick to everything. Whenever they return from a long hike, their Mom and grandparents always comment on how the smell of sage is all over their clothes and hair. They don't have this smell in their neighborhood back at home and appreciate it now. Danny looks up and down the street, and for the hundredth time, marvels at the lack of sidewalks on any of the streets. People here just walk on the shoulders of the roads, and that seems to work well enough. Grandma and Grandpa hear the car, and have come out on the front porch to greet everyone, with hugs and kisses all around. Danny and Wayne make their way into the front room, and the smells of this old house assault them. There are musty old wood, and cherry tobacco smells from Uncle Arvin's pipe, mostly—with other delicious food smell lingering from the last meal. Mom's grandfather built this house a hundred years ago, and now it creaks from well-worn age with every step taken. The boys see their Aunt Louise and Uncle Steve sitting at the dining room table, so wave and say Hi, and then plant themselves on the couch (what the adults call the Davenport), while Mom and Dad, Grandma and Grandpa join Louise and Steve at the table. The dining room table is at the other end of this single large room. The Davenport separates the one large room into two virtual rooms (dining room and living room). An old Wurlitzer organ pushes back against the Davenport. Grandpa and Mom play it well; the boys just make noise. The adults start visiting with one another as they play "Marbles." The game was already in progress when we arrived. Grandpas made this board out of heavy wood, years before, by wood-burning the indentations which support the marbles into the wood; with the distinct coloring for the four players added to the holes afterwards. The adults take turns playing the game, which involves rolling two die, and moving their colored marbles around the board.

 The boys hear their Grandpa ask, "Chinese Checkers, or just plain old checkers?"

 The others say that Marbles is acceptable. The news is on TV, which soon bores the boys, so they leap up and ask if they can go out and play.

 Grandma says, "The Hathaway's comes on at 8 o'clock, and that's in an hour."

 From Dad, "It'll soon be dark. Stay close to the house. Don't go out of site of the house."

 Grandpa says, "Watch out for snakes and tarantulas. Remember that the tarantulas come out towards evening. You already know that snakes come out in the evening too."

Grandma says, "Don't play on the stone wall out front either. You know there are Black Widow's in between the stones of that wall."

Both boys stand patiently and nod their heads often. They have had to listen to this speech many times and know they will have to hear it many times more. They have no intention of going near snakes, and will only hurt a tarantula if there is an ant hill nearby. Several months before, the boys discovered that if they hit a tarantula with a rock, and moved it with a stick to a large red ant hill, they could get many hours of enjoyment watching the ants dismantle the enormous spider and carry it down into their hole…bon appétit ants. At the very least, the boys would go off to play somewhere else, then stop by often to see how much progress the ants had made. Nature fascinates the boys in its simplicity; kill or be killed. Lives are so short-lived in nature. It never occurs to Danny or Wayne that the ants would never have had this meal without the wounding or killing, and subsequent serving of the spider to the ants. Both boys are passing through the front door.

Grandma and Mom both shout in unison, "Don't slam the screen door!"

But of course, it is too late, because all can hear the screen door slam.

There is a second delay before both boys yell from the other side of the door, "Sorry!"

We follow the boys down the three steps at the side of the porch, past the front bumper of their grandparent's station wagon, then into the empty lot beyond. This area has always been an exciting place to play because it is close to the house, but also passes for wilderness. Most of Southern California is desert and has been gradually converted to cultivated and populated space. All Southern Californian's know deep down that they have only tamed the desert. The desert is still there; has just been covered up, waiting to reclaim what it once had. It is always trying to change back into what it once was. The boys may be young, but they perceive that their grandparent's nice lawn is only green because they have to water it regularly. In this vacant lot just a few feet away, everything is dirt and sand, with the occasional weed (usually stickers, which are a barefoot boy's nemesis), and the occasional tumbleweed which the boy's love because of the connection to old westerns. They have no idea where tumble-weeds come from since they have never seen a green plant or bush that looks like a tumble-weed, and this just adds to the mystery of this place. The boys roam the area of the lot and look for snakes, tarantulas, or ants, and find the one large red ant mound they know of. They stare down at the huge ants with a mixture of fascination and revulsion.

Danny says, "If we go get the gas can in Grandpa's shed some time, we can pour the gas on the ants, then light it with a match."

Wayne says, "Why would you want to hurt the ants?"

Danny responds, "We kill spiders and tarantulas, don't we?"

Wayne, in his "young boy" wisdom replies, "Spiders don't have babies."

Danny knows he will not get support from Wayne on this, which is alright, so he is willing to do this alone. In fact, he is pretty excited about what will happen.

Mom yells from the porch, "Boys, Rocky Road ice cream!"

The boys don't delay at all, but race each other back to the house... the annihilation of an ant city temporarily forgotten. They enter into the house behind their Mom, and walk into the kitchen, where their Rocky Road ice cream has already been served into the thin metal bowls, and the boys like so much. Danny grabs the red bowl, his current favorite color. Wayne grabs the blue bowl, and both boys go back to their respective places on the Davenport. "Speedy Alka-Seltzer" is singing and dancing on the TV, and the boys wonder what Alka-Seltzer is. A car commercial from Los Angeles follows this commercial. The boys love these commercials. The guy named Cal is crazy, always having tigers or seals or monkeys pretending to be his dog Spot. No elephants or monkeys on this one. The guy has a snake, named Spot.

Danny turns to Wayne and comments, "I wanted to see the roller-skating monkey!"

Dad says, "Knock it off, the show is starting."

Both boys immediately quiet down. Dad is a stickler for silence from his boys when something is on TV. The boys especially love this show; a man and woman have three chimps for kids. Danny and Wayne wish they could have a chimp, but their parents say no. Dad even said a dirty word when he responded, "They crap all over the place!" Dad forgets his kids are around sometimes and says cuss words. One of the funniest things Dad does is when he sneezes. Instead of saying, "Ahhh-chooo!" like most people, he says, "Ahhhhh-shinola!" (Only it wasn't shinola). What makes this funnier to the boys is when after he does this, Mom gets embarrassed and tells him to stop doing that, and he replies that he can't help it; it just happens. The boys laugh at this because what are the odds that a person's sneeze will just randomly end in a sound which sounds like what he says? As everyone finishes their ice cream, all we can hear is the sound of metal spoons scraping on metal bowls. Danny and Wayne are stirring their ice cream with their spoons, getting it to melt and turn into what they call, "paint," so they can drink it down. At this exact moment, at this exact location… life is perfect. It is just after eight the next morning, when as if by magic, Danny and Wayne both wake up at the same time, and still in their pajamas, leave their bedroom and enter the front room. As always, their grandparents are already up. Grandma is in the kitchen getting a cup of coffee, and when she sees the boys she smiles.

She says, "Good morning Danny and Jerry. Did you sleep well?"

"Yes Grandma," both boys respond.

"Your Grandpa's down in the basement painting while it's still cool," she says

"Would you like some milk, while I put on breakfast?"

"Yes please!"

Both boys take their seats at the kitchenette near the back door. They love this time of the morning; and their personal time with their grandparents.

As if reading their minds, Grandma says, "I like this quiet time in the morning. Your Mom and Dad may be asleep for a while, since your Dad has worked so much overtime. You have to remember to be as quiet as you can, OK?"

Both boys are happy to comply and nod their heads. They love this woman.

Grandma sets their glasses in front of them; the red for Danny, and the blue for Wayne (she always remembers). She then starts to pull out all the ingredients she will need to make pancakes; flour, salt, baking powder, etc.

They both say, "Pancakes!"

They whisper this to prove to their Grandma they know how to listen.

"No, we're having waffles. You're close," she says with a smile.

Both boys now watch their Grandma busy about the kitchen, frying bacon, and making the waffles. They stare with fascination (and hunger), and before they know it their milk is finished, and over an hour has passed. Their Grandpa, following some internal clock, no doubt, knowing that breakfast would be ready, comes in through the back door, after ascending the steps from the basement. Within a few minutes Mom and Dad walk into the dining room, and the quiet time of the morning is over. Eddie is screaming from his carrier, which is set down on the floor, at the end of the dining room table.

"Good morning, Mom. I need to heat a bottle for Eddie. Are you through with the stove?"

"Of course, Honey. You know you don't ever have to ask."

Amazement covers the boys faces that first their Grandpa, then their parents, knew the exact time breakfast would be ready. They don't yet understand the power that the smell of coffee and bacon has on the unconscious mind. In Grandpa's case, he remembers that Grandma told him to come back upstairs at nine o'clock for breakfast. Grandma is old-fashioned in that she doesn't believe in buying things she can make herself. She makes the waffle batter from scratch, and she also makes the syrup from scratch. Danny especially loves watching her when she makes the syrup. She boils water and starts to pour in massive amounts of sugar which magically disappears as soon as she pours it. She adds no flavoring; not any maple flavoring. Grandma doesn't even let the sugared water cool down, so it can thicken up to the consistency of regular syrup. Grandma pours the pan contents into a gravy boat and places it on the table. Because the liquid is scathingly hot, an adult pours it onto the boy's waffles. The syrup is so hot, two surprising things happen: (1) The butter that was just painstakingly applied disappears altogether, and (2) The syrup itself is rapidly absorbed into the waffle (or pancake) with no sign of it anywhere. No syrup pools on top or the edges of the plate. As the sugar was magically absorbed into the water, so is the syrup absorbed into the waffle. This Fait Accompli is the perfect finishing touch to Grandma's secret. Grandpa is now talking about having to go shopping at the store, and Grandma and Mom agree that they would like to go, since Dad and the boys will be out hiking. They say both prayers before each meal (The one Grandma and Grandpa Say, and the one Mom and Dad, and family say):

"Come Lord Jesus, be our guest, let these, thy guests to us be blessed. Amen"

And, "Thank you for the world so sweet, thank you for the food we eat, thank you for the birds that sing, thank you God for everything. Amen".

During breakfast, the adults talk, but the boys don't. With the boys, when they eat, that's all they do. As breakfast finishes, the adults stay at the table to visit, while the boys go back to their bedrooms to put on their clothes. They do this quickly because adventures can be lost if they wait.

As they once again enter the dining room, Dad says, "I think we'll all go on a hike later. Sound like a good idea?"

The boys shout, "Yes", as the adults laugh at their excitement.

"Start thinking about where you'd like to go. We can hike to the hills where we can roll the tires down the hill. Or, we can hike up into Railroad Canyon. Or, we can hike down to the lake. Think about it."

The boys are nodding, knowing they are to, actually think about it, and not answer now.

"Go outside, and play for a while. Your Dad has to get ready. Stay within sight of the house."

Dad delivers this last with a stern look. The boys go out the front door; this time remembering to, not slam the screen doors. They stand very still side-by-side on the front porch. Danny knows that his Dad will be a while before he is ready, so they have enough time for Danny's proposal. Danny also knows that since Grandpa is going shopping, he will not be going back down to the basement to paint. This is excellent news because Danny needs to get the gas can out of the shed, and Grandpa would catch him if he were going down the back stairs.

Danny turns to look at Wayne and says, "I'm going to go burn the ants. Are you coming?"

"You need a match."

Danny responds to this statement by pulling a book of matches out of his pocket that he has taken from beside an ashtray in the front room. This is his Uncle Arvin's book of matches that he uses to light up his pipe when he visits. Danny is hoping the matchbook will not be missed before he can return it. Wayne doesn't even ask Danny where he got the matches. He knows Danny all too well; that he can improvise.

Wayne looks off into the empty field across the road in front of the house, and says, "No, I'm going to go look for diamonds or gold in that field."

Danny has expected this, and looking for diamonds and gold is a great pursuit; that almost changes his mind but Danny is stubborn.

He says, "OK, but come over if you change your mind."

Danny runs down the steps and walks quickly down the side of the house towards the back.

He freezes when he hears his Dad's booming voice yell, "Jean, where did you put my socks?"

This means that Dad is already in his bedroom which has a window he can look out of and see him. Danny knows that continuing his plans is extraordinarily dangerous, but to him it is well worth it. We, the witnesses, as always it seems, are with Danny; the feeling of mischief flows from him in thick waves. Danny pauses here for a moment, and then sprints to the side of the garage. There is no cover here, and no matter how small he makes himself, if someone looks out from the house, someone will see him. He is watching the back door, the windows, and the side of the house. He is soon brave enough and moves to the door on the shed-side of the garage. He fumbles with the hasp on the door for a few seconds, then steps into the musty, and old-smelling shed. He feels uncomfortable in here because of all the dust. Unusual objects (most of these are small glass jars with screw-top lids, which contain all kinds of things that he can identify; like screws and nails, but most of the items he has no idea what they are). He panics for a few moments because he can't find the gas can, and it suddenly comes into focus no more than two feet from his feet. He grabs it quickly (hoping there is no spider on the handle), turns around and scans the door and windows of the house one more time. Danny shuts the door with gas can in hand. He runs away from this area where it is too easy to be seen. He runs into the empty lot beside the house, and slows as he gets near the ants. He makes sure he doesn't accidentally stand where they can get on him. He decides to fill the main entrance hole with the gas, so leans over and begins to pour. Watching him do this, we see that he is very much into the moment, and has already forgotten how easy it would be for him to be discovered. He is in the middle of an open field where he can be seen from the main road, and at least three houses; but he doesn't seem to care. He has the presence of mind to use only a third of the gas in the can, so his Grandpa will not notice. He sets the can aside and then pulls the book of matches from his pocket. With practiced skill, he pulls out a single match, lights it, then without any hesitation, throws it on the ant mound. The fire is better than he imagined; it is burning much fiercer than he thought it would. He soon notices something totally unexpected. The ants that were out away from the mound are now running back to the mound and into the flames. We can learn from the look on Danny's face that he is totally lost on the meaning of this. The concept of suicide is unknown to him, so he can make no sense out of it at all. Totally beyond Danny's ability to comprehend is the basic fact that these ants aren't committing suicide, but instead, are doing whatever it takes, even in this hopeless situation, to keep their family from dying. This disturbs Danny on some level, by what he is seeing. Not because he feels sorry for the sacrificing ants, but because he doesn't understand why they are giving up their lives. He can't watch any longer, so runs back to the shed, to put the gas back. He closes and sets the hasp on the door, and walks back over to the stairs on the back porch where he sits down. He glances over at the field and sees that the flames are starting to die down, and that is good. Danny is giving the ants a lot of thought, and finally decides that they must be defective in some way. Nothing else makes sense to him. They had to see the fire, and even feel the heat from it, but still ran into the flames to be burnt to death. Danny has his hands in his pockets and feels the book of matches, and an idea seizes him. Danny has already forgotten about the ants, or any lessons he may learn. He hops up and walks back out into the empty lot. He keeps walking past the "barely burning" ant mound without even pausing to look down at the last of the martyrs, as they sacrifice their little ant lives in desperate futility. Danny reaches the edge of this lot and catty-corner from it is another vacant lot, which for some reason, he has never fully understood, has long, sun-dried grass (not like the desert that covers all other unoccupied space). He walks up to the edge of this grass, pulls out a match, lights it, then drops it into the grass. The fire starts to crackle and spread immediately, but Danny has already anticipated this. He stomps out the fire before it has a chance to grow larger. As soon as he stomps out this fire, he starts another one, stomps it out, and starts another. What we can see, but Danny is missing, is that, in the areas that he stomps out, small coals and embers are still glowing. Danny is now more than ten feet away from where he started, when an area near where he started flares up, and without him there to stomp out, spreads quickly. Right after we notice, so does Danny. He runs back and starts stomping, but the fire has grown too fast. As soon as he realizes the situation is out of his control, he runs back to his grandparent's house at a dead run. He goes in slowly, trying to act nonchalant, so the adults will suspect nothing. Danny sees that Wayne is already inside. Too many people around for him to put the matches back, so after he sits down, he slips them under the cushion where he is sitting.

 About five minutes later, Danny and Wayne sit next to each other on the couch, and stare at a blank TV screen (This was normal in this household. The TV is on during evenings only…or sometimes for the grandchildren's cartoons in the morning. It is too much of a distraction to be left on all the time). They are listening to their Mom and grandparents talk behind them while their Dad is finishing up getting ready in the back bedrooms. In the distance, they hear a siren; first by the boys with their outstanding young hearing, then by Mom, and finally the grandparents. When Danny and Wayne first hear it, they look at each other.

Danny is thinking, "Oh no!"

Wayne is thinking, "What did you do now?"

Mom says, "I hope nobody's hurt."

Grandpa says, "We haven't had any rain for some time. I hope it's not a fire."

As if in reply to Grandpa's statement, a second siren starts to wail in the distance, adding its voice to that of the first.

"Oh, no…that's a police car, and a fire truck," Grandpa says.

Mom asks, "How can you tell?"

"Do you hear the deeper sound of the fire truck? It almost sounds like a truck horn."

Danny is staring at the blank TV in front of him and is watching the ghosts of the adults. This is an illusion he discovered a while ago; if he makes his eyes go out of focus a little, he can barely make out their shapes. He knows where they are sitting, so he knows who the shapes are. He isn't able to see facial expressions, exactly, but he can see when they look at each other, and when they look at him. Suddenly, there is the sound of a second fire truck, and now they can hear the first two vehicles making the turn on to their street and coming their way.

Grandpa says, "Oh no, that must be a neighbor's house," as he stands and starts to walk towards the front door.

The women have also stood up, and are joining Grandpa. They all go through the door, and on to the front porch, just in time to see the police car (a black and white 1958 Chevy Delray with red lights flashing on the roof) go by with the fire truck (a flat red Dennis 1959 F28) right behind. Both vehicles are slowing as they pass in front, which is not a good sign. All three adults are now moving off the front porch towards the direction of the approaching emergency vehicles and the vacant lot next door, and as they come off the porch, the smell of fire hits them, and they see the thick smoke filling the air. Wayne is right behind the adults, but the adults will recall later that Danny is suspiciously absent.

All four of them are now running behind the vehicles on a diagonal towards where they see the empty field beyond totally engulfed in flames. The next thing they see is the ten or more neighbors who are now trying desperately to put out the flames with shovels, rakes, and brooms, but are losing the battle. Beyond the flames, are the homes they are all trying so desperately to protect. The fire truck stops just short of the fire; and firemen jump out and start readying the hose. A second fire truck (exactly like the first), siren wailing, slows and makes the turn across the lot, pulling up next to the first truck, with the firemen jumping off and running before the vehicle came to a complete stop. Two police officers get out of their car and start running towards the neighbors on the other side of the flames. Dad, who also hears the sirens, finishes tying his shoes, and has run out of the house, not even noticing Danny at the window, then runs down to be with Mom and her parents. All adults (and Wayne hiding behind Mom and peeking around her), watch as the two officers approach one person at a time, trying to get their attention with lots of yelling and pointing. The neighbors respond with exaggerated shakes of their heads while continuing to try to put out the flames in front of them. Some firemen carrying shovels run to where the neighbors are, and start working at their sides. Seeing the firemen are better clothed and equipped for such a struggle, the neighbors finally realize the danger they are in and one-by-one, start to back off. By now the hoses from the two fire trucks are spraying from the other side and are finally gaining ground on the fire. We have not been outside with Mom and Dad, her parents, and her son. We are standing behind Danny, as he is standing at the window in the dining room, watching all of the action. He has a weird facial expression, which we cannot read. No, we saw this same look just a while ago when he was watching the ant martyrs. The neighbors are also braving a fire to protect their homes, instead of running away as Danny would have expected. Are they martyrs too? If only we could hear his thoughts. We realize for the first time that maybe even Danny doesn't know what drives him. Maybe he isn't the master planner we have thought him to be; but instead, he is fumbling through life acting on every whim or impulse. Perhaps it is a combination of both. In the distance, we see that the firemen with the hoses continue to spray the charred remains of the field, even though the flames have long been extinguished. The two police officers are now walking from neighbor to neighbor asking them questions. Mom and Dad and her parents (and Wayne lagging behind), have wandered over to the burned ground where they can be seen having animated conversations with the neighbors. The police officers walk to their car, climb in and away they drive. Evidently the Police Officers were unable to find the person or persons who started the fire. Danny sighs when this happens, and a depression settles over him that he doesn't get to talk to the officers. All of the neighbors have formed a circle around Mom and company, and now an intriguing thing happens. Like God Himself has announced the guilty party, they all turn as one, then start pointing towards the house where Danny stands. Danny flinches back in surprise. How could they have seen him from where they are? What should he do now? He takes a chance and peeks out the window again and sees the large group marching across the field towards him. Danny barely registers the firemen beyond putting away the two hoses, and getting the scene cleaned up for their return to their station. Danny is frantic now. What should he do? Should he run? Should he try to hide? In the end, he realizes the futility of any such action so just stands remarkably still facing the front door. Danny didn't know what a mob is, but he takes a crash course in it now. His parents and grandparents are leading the way, followed by fifteen neighbors (it seems that other neighbors have seen the mob and decided to join it as it moves across the lot.)

Dad opens the door and locks eyes with him. "Get your butt out here now!"

Paralysis, born of fear of his Dad, grips Danny, and keeps him frozen in place. Dad moves towards him exceptionally fast for a big man, and picks him up by the back of his shirt, carrying him out the door.

"I told you to get your butt out here!"

A particularly strong and heavy hand comes down on Danny's butt to emphasize this last statement. Dad sets Danny down on the porch, while keeping a hand rested on his shoulder from behind. Mom and her parents stand-off to the side, back behind Dad. All of Danny's accusers form a half-circle around them. It appears this is a tribunal, and Danny is not the only one on trial. Everyone has heard of the phrase "Guilt by association", and boy, are they associated. The oldest man in the group, looking to be Grandpa's age (and sadly, before this moment, a good friend of Grandpa), steps forward and speaks to Danny.

He says, "My Martha was out watering her plants when she saw you sneaking around in that field; right before the fire."

"I saw him carrying a gas can before that," says a portly redheaded woman.

The old man continues, "Do you deny it was you that did this?"

Danny stands very calmly, staring at a crack in the sidewalk, in front of him.

The old man again, "Speak up Boy!"

Dad starts to bear down on Danny's shoulder and gives it a squeeze which isn't quite gentle. Embarrassment floods over Dad; and he can be extraordinarily danger when embarrassed. An old woman with blue-gray hair up in a bun, and wearing a light-green pantsuit, steps forward, with eyes fixed on the ground in front of Danny—or, so it seems. All turn to watch her until she gets about five feet from him and stops.

She says, "What happened to your shoes?"

All eyes look down, and they see what caught Mabel Zimmerman's attention; a white pair of tennis shoes, with black rings surrounding the bottom inch or so.

Danny is also staring down, with a stupid look that says, "Wow, I never thought of that!"

Dad reaches down, lifts Danny's knee up on his right leg with one hand, and pulls his shoe off with the other one. He raises the shoe up to his nose and takes a deep smell. Dad says, "It smells like charcoal."

Dad shakes his head and backs away, as if he is so disappointed, he will not provide protection to this boy any longer.

A woman's voice yells, "I vote we all spank him!"

"Yes!"

"He deserves it!"

"We could have lost our homes!"

Without permission from the parents or grandparents (but something like quiet consent from them anyway), the mob advances. As a mother gives a doctor implied permission to give her child a shot, or whatever is necessary…because in the end, the doctor always knows best, the mob advances. Besides, this is for the best, isn't it? Danny is now alone with these strangers and feels that his family has abandoned him. He looks from one parent to the other, pleading with them, but all he gets in return is cold stares. He looks to his grandparents, and he gets the same look from his Grandma and Grandpa; but his Grandpa looks away after a few seconds. Unknown hands grab Danny's wrists. His pants are unbuttoned and pulled down to his ankles. Now, Danny is embarrassed and his face flames a bright red. He looks around briefly, and sees that more neighbors have flocked here. Like vultures to carrion, they have come to watch the entertainment. He can see kids of all ages laughing and pointing at him. The first person's hand descends and lands on his bottom, which brings him back to the reality of the moment. The adults up front, the ones who feel they have more owed them because their homes were at risk, are deadly serious. The fire badly frightens them, and they will get their pound of flesh if it takes all day. As each person takes his or her turn in succession, Danny hears these people speaking as folks talking about the weather will, with no emotion.

"Three hits apiece, then move aside and let the next person have his turn."

"No pushing, everyone gets a turn."

"Hold him, he's starting to squirm."

Danny is in a nightmare from which he cannot awaken. He can't decide which is worse: the inner circle of adults he has wronged, doling out their punishment with grim efficiency, or the outer circle of spectators creating a carnival-like atmosphere. The outer circle people are even sitting on his grandparent's stone wall, as if they own it. This violates some personal ownership ethic Danny has, and bothers him more than the beating he is receiving. Another thing he has been somewhat aware of, that he now starts to focus on, is that his spankers are talking to him while they deliver their justice.

They are saying things like, "I'll bet you never set fires again!"

And

"I hope you have learned your lesson!"
And
"I hate having to do this, but you've made me!"

Danny looks over his shoulder at his first woman tormentor just once, and decides he has no interest in doing so again. Once she starts her hand swinging, she gets into the thrill of this moment, and leaves her calm and efficient demeanor behind, and picks up an entirely different personality. She has a crazy wildness in her eyes (a craving, a hunger) which now controls her, shoving her thinking-self to some unreachable place. Danny remembers how a guard dog once charged a cyclone fence he was walking past, and behind the snarling, and foaming mouth, the thing that scared him the most was the ferocious, and reptilian-looking strangeness in the dog's eyes. Her eyes are like that for the few seconds he looks at her. Danny decides to close his eyes to make the rest of his punishment more bearable…if that is possible.

The speaker of the mob, who has held Danny's hands through all of this, is now last and says, "Here, someone hold his wrists."

He hits Danny three times, maybe harder than the others, but Danny can't tell. His bottom is so on fire now, he is trying as hard as he can to not scream, or cry. He doesn't want to give any of these people the satisfaction. After the last swing, the leader walks around to Danny's front and leans over.

He says, "I better never see you again anywhere near my house, or I'll give you a whipping within an inch of your life! With a belt! See if I don't."

He now stands up and looks at all the "insiders".

He says, "If you ever come anywhere near any of our houses again, we will whip you!"

He looks up at Dad and says, "You better keep your kids on a leash. Those boys got no supervision. You let em' run wild as these do, they're bound to get up to no good."

Dad has decided that this situation has moved past discipline and into verbal abuse, and will not stand for it. He starts to move forward but his Father-in-law's hand grabs his shoulder from behind, and he can hear a whispered, "Wait," from behind.

Dad stops with a monumental effort on his part. Like control from a single mind, the mob turns as one and moves to the stairs at the end of the porch. They don't make a sound as if they are suddenly wondering to themselves, "what the hell just happened?" The outer circle people, suddenly realizes the show is over and wander off in search of entertainment elsewhere. Danny is still standing unusually still, pants at his ankles. Danny has red marks around his wrists where held by hands too strong for far too long, for one so young. His bottom and backs of his thighs flame with bright-red marks and welts; where over-zealous adults have just overreacted, with too much emotion on a small and defenseless boy. His injuries are stinging and throbbing with pain, but a totally unexpected sense of calm has descended over him. His head is down, and just a few tears are flowing down his cheeks, but he is proud of himself, that it is just these few. Mom bends over and pulls up his pants, being especially gentle when she gets them up to his thighs and bottom. Mom leads Danny into the house, with Grandma following them. Mom and Grandma are speaking softly to him, as if they are in a hospital. Dad and Grandpa stay on the porch and watch the fire trucks as they move up out of the lot and on to the road in front of them. These trucks are just trucks now—no sirens, and in no hurry now. Two of the firemen hanging off the back of the first truck, turn and stare at them with accusing looks. They suspect word got around pretty quick where the offender lived.

Grandpa says, "Thanks for restraining yourself, Buck. I know it wasn't easy. The fella that did all the talking is John Rose. John is on the city council, so he has many supporters around here. I've been trying to get his approval for recognizing my Sleeping Giant painting."

"I don't follow you."

"You know the painting I'm talking about?"

Dad nods his head and says, "Yes. That's one of your best ones. I love that one."

Grandpa continues, "I came up with the idea a while back that if they use my Sleeping Giant for tourism, it can be a way to draw in visitors. Everyone would come to Elsinore and use a picture of my painting on a tourism pamphlet, to be able to make out the head, body, and feet of the giant in the Ortega Mountains."

Dad is now making eye contact with his Father-in-law.

He asks, "Don't tell me, Danny just pissed off the very person who was going to approve or disapprove your proposal?"

Grandpa doesn't say anything, just stares off into the distance, looking at nothing in particular.

Mom yells from inside, "Buck? Dad?"

Dad says, "It will still work out OK. Nothing was permanently damaged. This will all be water under the bridge."

Dad gives grandpa a pat on the shoulder then they both go inside. Mom and Grandma are sitting at the dining room table and are motioning the men to sit down.

Grandma says, "We need to talk about this."

Grandpa says, "Yes Dear, we do. Where's Danny?"

Mom says, "I laid him down for a nap. He had quite an emotional experience, and I think he can use the rest."

Mom lowers her head as if remembering even a part of what just happened is too much for her to bear. Wayne sits alone on the Davenport staring at the blank screen watching the adults as they discuss this terrible day, but also as they discuss what needs to be done about Danny…and his influence on Wayne. Because things can always get worse…they do. Eddie once again starts to scream and does so for an awful long time. Out on the road, an orange (with white top) 1957 Chevy convertible with the top rolled back, and the windows rolled down, and radio blasting, cruises by. Wayne looks out the window admiring it as it creeps by. The car has just been washed, because the chrome is so bright it catches the sun and makes him squint. To Wayne, the car looks like a 50/50 bar, those orange and vanilla ice creams they always get when they go to the drive-in. The front windows are rattling from the loudness of the song, "It's gonna work out fine," by Ike and Tina Turner.

Friends

In October of 1962, Mom and Dad stayed glued to the TV watching every event of the Cuban Missile Crisis. The thought that the United States was on the verge of World War Three, frightens everyone. Dad talked about what they should do as a family, to survive. Should they flee to the mountains? Would they be safe from nuclear fallout there? How far would they need to get away from the Los Angeles area, to be safe? Thoughts of extended family in other towns and cities caused renewed anxiety. How can they all be protected from harm? Dad knows of other people who have bomb or fallout shelters built into their backyards, and wishes they had one now. All of the grocery stores had already been cleaned out, just days into the crisis. Mom and Dad were fortunate to get all they need before everything was gone. In the trunk of the car, are plenty of canned foods, jugs of water, and suitcases for everyone, and camping equipment. They are ready to go at a moment's notice, but so are millions of their neighbors. Dad knows they should have left days ago, to avoid the clogged roads…not that they have a safe destination in mind. Many people have already fled to the mountains and the desert, and they talk about confrontations daily; some ending in shootings. In the end, Dad decides that they should just ride this out since they wouldn't have time to get away from the "kill zone". Danny, of course, is taking this all in, but doesn't yet have the necessary coping skills or the ability to figure out how to deal with his feelings. To him, a nuclear bomb is like the biggest and meanest monster a person could ever run into. How can such a thing exist? Danny puts nuclear bombs in his "things that don't belong" list, like; the gigantic pine tree, Green Valley, and the witch's house. The holocaust is fully averted within the next few days, but this situation has affected Danny forever. It is the first time where not only he has faced something utterly out of his control, but also everyone he knows (and doesn't know), within entire areas. To realize for the first time that whole cities (people, animals, trees, buildings…everything) can be snuffed out in a moment fills him with hopelessness, and despair. Danny sat there with his family and watched all of the post-WWII nuclear disaster movies, but he never took them seriously. From now on, he will watch these types of movies from new eyes, and believe everything they say. From now on, Danny will feel as if he is not just a spectator, but also one of the characters; whatever happens to them can and will happen to him.

2

Time slips forward, four months. It is February of 1963. Danny is now four and a half, Wayne is just over three, Eddie is a year and nine months, and Mom is six months pregnant, with her fourth child. She will soon have four children, with less than five years between the oldest and youngest, and she shudders at the thought. Since the fire in Elsinore, Danny has once again "Gone to ground." He still skulks in the shadows, and makes Mom worry about the way he acts when she comes upon him; like catching him doing something wrong. At least, there haven't been any life and death situations…Thank God. She does hear Danny and Wayne screaming at each other back in their bedroom, or outside, but when she goes to see what is going on, they are always perfectly innocent boys. It is almost like they have a sixth sense of where she is, at all times. Danny and Wayne have started going their own ways more and more recently. She would like for them to stay together for strength in numbers, but she knows all too well what happens if they are with each other too much. They have their own friends too, and are spending more time away from each other. Either they are at a friend's house, or friends are here, getting under foot. Danny seems to collect friends as Mom used to collect S & H Green Stamps. It is not uncommon for Danny to have all of his friends in the backyard (or in the house) at once. Mom once counted eleven of Danny's friends in the back yard. Today, she went out to ask Danny something and couldn't find him anywhere. She asked each of his friends (boys and girls) where he might be found. They all said Danny went to their houses one-by-one and told them he was inviting them over for a party. Once they were all assembled here, Danny had disappeared. Mom told them they could all go home, and waited for Danny to come home, so she could ask him, "What in the name of Sam Hill are you doing?" We, the witnesses have been walking behind Danny during all of these hikes and have been wondering the same thing. He has just left a girl in his backyard and is once again moving quickly down the alley towards some unknown destination. He never hesitates but knows exactly where he is going, like someone who has traveled these streets for longer than he has been alive. An Ice Cream Truck goes by with that repeating play-until-you-go-crazy tune, and Danny doesn't even glance that way. We have just settled in for a long walk when Danny turns left and walks up to a side gate of a single-story house (which looks so much like all the other homes in this neighborhood). He doesn't announce himself, just walks into the backyard and on to the back porch. A boy his own age is sitting in a field of toys; making this place look more like an amusement park. There are army men, *Tinker Toys*, *Lincoln Logs*, *Erector Sets*, toy cars, and toy trucks. There are toy planes, and toy jeeps, an *Etch-a-sketch*, and a red *AstroRay* gun that shoots darts. Danny also sees one of his favorites, *Mouse Trap*, which absolutely fascinates him. He decides he will play that one first. Danny says, "Hi Johnny."

Johnny turns to him and asks, "Where are they?"

"They're at my house. They won't bother us now. We can play all by ourselves."

The fact that Danny was accomplishing all of this work for a relatively innocent purpose, relieves us, but also bothers us by the lengths Danny will go through, to get his way. We find chairs on the periphery of the patio and sit down to wait for Danny to be on the move again, but it looks as if he may be here for some time.

Johnny says, "Danny, look at this. It's a new toy. I got a Wham-O Air Blaster Gun. It has a Gorilla target. Look!"

He produces an ugly-looking all-black gun that looks like a Thompson Machine Gun.

"Isn't it bitchin?" Johnny glances to his right to make sure his Mom hasn't overheard him.

Danny replies, "That is so boss, lemme see it!"

Of course, Danny loves it. Instead of using the Gorilla target, however, the boys spend their time firing the puffs of air this thing generates, on each other; hair, ears, face, etc.

At just past five, which is a few hours later, Johnnie's Mom sticks her head out of the back door and says,

"Danny, it's time to go home now."

Danny nods once and leaves the way he came. There are no sloppy goodbyes between him and his friend. This is like a business relationship, and now their business is over. We follow Danny home, but now he is walking more slowly; not in such a hurry. Maybe he is wondering what he will tell all of the kids he left in his backyard… maybe not. A 1955 "Pepto Bismol" pink and white Ford Fairlane Crown Victoria, cruises by, and, "Travelin' Man," by Ricky Nelson, is playing on the radio.

The Art of the Punch and Falling

It is the following Saturday, and Danny and Wayne (and now Eddie), are up early as is usual, watching cartoons. Their parents will sleep for another hour (maybe, or until the boys get hungry and go to wake them up). Being the oldest, Danny always wakes up Dad. This involves walking into his parent's bedroom quietly (Inga, who sleeps in his parent's bed sometimes growls or barks, and sometimes doesn't), then raising one of Dad's eye-lids, bending down to look deeply into the center of his eye.

Danny asks, "Dad, are you awake?"
Dad responds, "I am now."
Danny says, "We're hungry."

Dad will then do his part, and buy breakfast, or have Mom make breakfast; either way, he feeds everyone, and Dad is happy. As is the case almost every Saturday for months now, and probably from now on, Danny and Wayne have started to fight. The arguments start small with some words said over which cartoon they should watch (which is a common argument). On this morning, Danny decides to kneel next to the TV with his hand on the channel changer. To provoke Wayne further, he randomly changes the channels, saying things like, "How about this one? Yes? Oh, too bad. Not that one."

EDEN FADING

After a few minutes of this teasing, Wayne has finally had enough and says, "Keep it on Tennessee Tuxedo!"

Danny changes the channel. Wayne stands up and reaches for the channel with his hand, which Danny bats away. Now Wayne tries a fake to the left to throw Danny off-balance, but Danny's hand stays on the channel. Danny leans back hard the other way and leaves himself unbalanced which Wayne now takes advantage of by pushing his shoulder in the direction Danny is moving. This causes Danny to fall flat on his stomach with a distinct karate-sound that involuntarily escapes from his lungs. Wayne reaches in above Danny, changes the channel back to Tennessee Tuxedo, then runs back to the couch where he plops back down.

Eddie screams, "Yakkety Yak!" with unrestrained glee.

This is a character on Tennessee Tuxedo that Eddie particularly likes.

Danny is still lying there, but has turned to face Wayne and says, "That hurt! You are so going to get it. I am going to pound you!"

Wayne sits there in rapt fascination with Tennessee and his friend Chumley, totally oblivious to his taunting brother. Danny stands up and walks over to the couch. He spins his back towards the couch as if he is just about to sit down (which causes Wayne to visibly relax), then Danny straightens out and swings his fist, connecting solidly with Wayne's arm. There are two punches we have seen the boys use on each other (because their parents have strictly forbidden stomach, groin, or head punches). These are:

(1) The arm punch, which is the boy's favorite because it requires no setup and is easily delivered.

(2) The back punch, which is more difficult on the setup, because the victim is usually running away from the puncher.

On chance occasions (for unknown reasons to the giver of the punch), the victim spins his back towards you. The coup de grâce is always the back hit. If done right; make your hand into a fist, raise it high above your head with your thumb pointing towards the deliverer, bringing it out and down in a closed-hand karate chop into the top-dead-center of the victim's back (right between the shoulder blades), is a tremendous event. The puncher will not only get his victim to scream and bend backwards while bending their elbows back behind them; you will also hear the deep, resonating drum-like boom made because of the air in the lungs. With every back hit administered to a brother, there is always an attempt to make it the best blow ever, which is always tested by the size of the boom. The brother who administers this hit usually only has a few seconds to gloat, because as soon as the receiver recovers sufficiently, he is now on the offensive, and the last hitter is now on the run. This role-reversal with the hitting happens every time the boys are alone, like this Saturday morning. After Danny punches Wayne, he stands back and looks menacingly at his brother; as if he is ready to throw another punch if needed. Wayne lay's over on the couch, grimacing in pain and holding his arm. There is no crying between these two. Eddie is still young enough to cry, so his two older brothers have to be careful with him. They have to leave him alone for fear of waking their parents. Instead, Wayne starts to breathe hard—sounding like an old steam train pulling out from a station, and picking up speed. From experience, whenever Wayne starts to breathe this way, he becomes unusually aggressive, to the point that he will charge Danny with everything he has regardless of what he is getting back. Danny believes in an orderly punishment system (controlled hit for controlled hit); not this windmill-style punching Wayne adopts when he gets angry. Danny knows he has a few seconds to retreat, so spins and runs for the back door. Wayne is right after him. Danny has to slow to open the back door, which is Wayne's opening, and the perfect setup for the back hit. Danny has taught him well, and he delivers the blow perfectly. Danny yells out, bends backwards, and falls to his knees. Wayne takes advantage of this opportunity and runs for the back door. Because Danny is now blocking the back door, Wayne sprints towards the deeper recesses of the house, looking for a place, to hide. Danny loves this game. The longer Wayne stays hidden, the angrier Danny will get, then the more the damage once he catches him. Danny thinks to himself, that Wayne should have learned a long time ago, that it is worse on him to keep delaying his punishment. He should just give up right away, instead of delaying the inevitable. Danny begins the hunt.

He is a patient and thorough hunter. He likes to fake as if he is going one way, then run low to the ground to hide behind furniture, thinking he will catch Wayne doubling back. Danny looks in the kitchen, then the dining room. Instead of sweeping towards the living room, as Wayne would expect, he runs back to the kitchen, but no luck. He now runs to the living room, and there's Eddie sitting peacefully on the couch still watching the cartoon. Danny walks slowly back to the bedroom, looking under beds and in the closet. He remembers that Wayne once went into their parent's room to hide; knowing that Danny would never think about going in there. Danny walks over to his parents room and puts his ear to the door listening. He hears the thudding of running bare feet to his right, and sees Wayne running into the living room from the bathroom. He chastises himself for forgetting to look there. He runs into the dining room, to cut Wayne off, but Wayne never comes. Keeping an eye on the hallway, and the living room in front of him, Danny walks slowly into the living room, just in time to hear Wayne running out the other entrance of the living room and into the hall. Danny spins to his left and sees the back of Wayne as he crosses towards the back door. He runs after Wayne, and renews the chase. Danny reaches the back door just as it closes from the outside. As soon as Danny is outside and down the stairs, he barely makes out Wayne as he ducks behind the playhouse at the back of the yard. Danny knows there are bikes stored between the playhouse and the fence, so Wayne will not be sneaking through there. He has just trapped himself…that idiot. Danny circles wide as a big cat cornering its prey. He rounds the last corner, and already has his fist raised, ready to deliver his punch, but his brother isn't there. Danny spins in place looking everywhere around him, not understanding where his brother could have gone. He suddenly realizes where he went. On the backside of the playhouse is a window several feet up; which Danny would have thought impossible for Wayne to climb. He stands on his tiptoes, with his hands on the sill and pulls himself up, but doesn't see his brother inside. Just then, there is a sound to Danny's left, so he drops and moves over to gaze into the space between the playhouse and brick wall. Wayne astonishes Danny, when Wayne comes out the other side. Wayne has somehow navigated his way over and around the maze of bikes and can now be seen running towards the walnut tree. Danny yells out in frustration, and then runs back the way he came; not wanting to waste time going through the bikes. He goes around the barbecue grill, and gets to the tree, just as Wayne is reaching for the top rung.

"I'm going to kill you! You better stop now!" Danny yells—not realizing (or caring) he is right outside his parent's room.

Wayne is silent, focusing on getting a tight hold on the wooden rung. Danny scales the ladder far faster than Wayne, and reaches the upper landing just as Wayne is climbing out on the large branch (that stretches out from the tree, and ends up over the playhouse, fifty feet from here). There are many smaller branches which grow left, right, and down off this main branch, but there is also a large one that grows straight up half-way out from the tree. Wayne is just reaching for this vertical branch to grasp (to swing around to the other side), when Danny catches up with him. It is a small push Danny gives him, which under normal circumstances, would be nothing. Up here in this tree, however, it is more than enough. There is no drama, where Wayne is struggling mightily to hang on, with Danny fighting to help or hinder (depending on his mood). One second Wayne has started his swing around the branch, and the next second he is falling. Danny stares after him with dumb fascination as he drops the fifteen feet to the ground. Danny can't believe what he is seeing. Wayne hits head first (so hard, he bounces), coming to rest on his stomach, with his hands at his sides. As Danny looks on, there is no movement from below. He turns and quickly runs back the way he came. He descends the rungs, and runs to Wayne's side. Danny bends down, so he can see Wayne's face.

He says, "Wayne? Are you OK?"

"Wayne?"

There is no answer, and no movement. Danny leans in closer and hears something. Wayne's lips are barely moving, as he says something. Danny puts his ear up next to Wayne's lips.

He hears him say, "Mommy, Mommy."

Wayne repeats this litany over and over. Danny stands and looks towards the back window of his parent's bedroom. He is torn by indecision. He knows he will get the blame for this, but he didn't do anything. Danny decides to go see if his Mom or Dad is awake yet. He quickly walks into the house, and to his parent's bedroom door. Dad startles him, as he walks out of the living room, with Inga trotting behind.

Dad says, "Hi Son, you need me for something? Were you, and Wayne outside? We told you not to leave Eddie by himself."

Dad finally is noticing how nervous Danny is, but before he can ask him why, Danny blurts out,

"Wayne fell from the tree and isn't moving."

Dad is immediately on the move towards the back door.

Dad yells, "Jean! Wayne fell from the tree, come quick!"

Danny follows in Dad's wake as he runs out the back door, crosses the yard, and kneels next to his second Son.

Wayne has not moved and is now speaking the mantra a little more loudly, "Mommy, Mommy."

Dad reaches down and gently rolls Wayne over on to his back cradling his head in his own lap. The back door slams as Mom comes running up to Dad and Wayne. We see Danny standing up against the house, near the back porch, watching.

Mom asks Danny, "Did I hear you say he fell out of the tree?"

She looks up to the branches far above. She has always hated the boys running through its branches, dreading something like this happening.

Dad says, "Danny told me Wayne fell out of the tree. I haven't had a chance to quiz him further yet. Probably playing grab-ass; like always."

Dad favors Danny with a disapproving look, while Wayne opens his eyes and stares back at his Dad.

"Are you OK Wayne?"

Wayne answers in a whisper, "My head hurts."

"Lift your left arm for me…Now wiggle your fingers. Now your right arm. Lift your left leg and move your foot around. Now move your right leg. Good."

Now Dad begins to feel Wayne's head very gently.

Looking at Danny, he asks, "How did he land on the ground?"

Danny doesn't answer his Dad right away, because he has been daydreaming.

Dad again, "I said; how did he land on the ground?"

"He fell on the ground from the tree. I …I didn't push him."

"Did I ask you if you pushed him? I asked you, did he land on his feet, his back?"

"He fell on his head."

Dad ignores Danny for now. He will take care of him later. He knows from experience this wasn't an accident. Just a few minutes ago, He and Jean were lying in bed talking about what they were going to do today when they heard the telltale clues that the boys were fighting: screaming and yelling, followed by the sound of running feet, then another yell, then running feet. Each loud noise elicits another growl from Inga. This pattern of noise can go on for a while until he and Jean emerge from their bedroom. When they come upon the boys they will see that anger flushes their faces, and exercise; usually breathing heavily. If he and Jean want to see which boys have been fighting, this is the first thing they look for. This time, however, the boys don't stay indoors. After a few minutes of silence they heard the back door slam shut twice, then after another few moments, they heard Danny yell from out back, "I'm going to kill you," which happens to be one of Danny's favorite things to yell. Dad sat up quickly and started to throw on a pair of pants, saying, "Oh Lord help us. Here we go again. We don't ask for much. Just give us one morning of peace."

Back in the present, Dad looks back to Wayne and asks, "Very slowly, try to move your head; just a bit."

Wayne moves his head slowly back and forth. Dad continues to feel Wayne's head for bumps, or maybe something more obvious (like a fracture). He finds just the one large "goose-egg" on the front-center of the top of his head.

"Let's get him in the house," says Mom.

Dad carefully supports Wayne, and slowly stands. Mom moves in next to Dad, and they advance together towards the house. As they pass where Danny remains standing, neither parent glances his way or says a word to him. As the door opens and closes, Danny stands where he is for a few more seconds. He then wanders over to sit at the picnic table to wait for his Dad. Before Danny sits down, he bends down to pick up a walnut—the big round, green walnuts (nothing like his Grandma gets during Christmas time that they sit around cracking with the nutcracker.

Inside the house, Dad lays Wayne on his bed, and Mom and Dad are leaning over him asking him questions. They would like to be able to take Wayne to the doctor, but they can't afford it because they don't have medical insurance with Dad's new job yet. Instead, they will take turns, keeping an eye on him. If he does get worse, or stops improving, Mom and Dad will take him to the hospital. Neither parent has the energy to grill Danny, or determine his punishment. Priorities first, and Danny isn't going anywhere. We are now in the back yard again, sitting across the table from Danny. We are still trying to figure out what makes him do the things he does; or why his reactions are always different from what we expect. He is bouncing the walnut off of the table in front of him, like a mini-basketball that's lost its air. He is doing this absently as he stares off at nothing in particular. We hear Danny whispering, and the prospect that he may provide a clue to his behavior excites us; something that will lead us to understanding. Perhaps, the complexity of his thoughts will shock us…the pure evil. We lean in to listen, "… Meet George Jetson, his boy Elroy, daughter Judy, Jane, his wife. "

Danny whispers while he throws the walnut at the fence, "I wish I was a Jetson…or a Flintstone."

The end of summer and Halloween arrives

Lee, 1963

In May of 1963 Mom gives birth to her fourth boy, Lee. Mom is glad she has a healthy baby, but terribly disappointed she didn't get her little girl. She was pregnant between Eddie and Lee but had a miscarriage *again*. It was a girl *again*. She and Buck decided that this is it; four boys are enough…especially after these boys. She will have to give up on her dream of having a girl. It is fascinating to see how the dynamics of the family change with the addition of each child. Danny is still the leader, but over time, Wayne has shown signs of being a partner, instead of just a follower. Eddie loved being the youngest and getting all of the attention, but now he's not the youngest any longer. To make it worse on Eddie (because he no longer has the full attention of Mom and Dad), he is now fair game for harm from Danny and Wayne. Danny now has two victims, and for the first time, Wayne has someone he can intimidate too. Mom and Dad immediately notice the difference between Eddie and Lee. Lee is happy all the time…Eddie, when he was this age, cried all the time…and still does. The new dynamic is intriguing but also keeps Mom and Dad busier than ever before. Instead of a linear progression in the degree of chaos with the addition of each boy, they are seeing a geometric progression. Instead of the fourth boy being four times more difficult than one, the fourth makes it 10 or 20 times more difficult.

2

It is the last week in August of 1963, and Danny starts school. He immediately hates everything about it; just as Emma had predicted. The start of school doesn't settle Danny down at all. In fact, because he is so frustrated to be somewhere he doesn't want to be, his anger ratchets up. The first weekend after Danny starts school, Aunt Rebecca and Uncle Gordo and their three daughters; Steph, Margaret, and Peggy visit. They are all out back while Dad and Gordo are cooking hamburger and hotdogs on the barbecue. Danny and Wayne have been wrestling and fighting for the last two hours, and nothing Mom or Dad have done including threats, spankings, and isolation has helped. They are so aggravated with each other it's just a matter of time before they hurt or kill each other. Dad turns to look for Danny and Wayne and sees them wrestling on the driveway. They are fighting in their usual style; punching, pinching, kicking, scratching, and biting. Dad calmly lays down his spatula, walks over to the boys, and grabs Danny off of Wayne. He carries Danny under his arm to the garage and then throws him up onto the roof. Danny lands on his butt, then scrambles to his feet for fear of bouncing or falling off. Danny stands there and solemnly watches from his birds-eye view as Dad strides back to where Wayne has been quietly sitting (it never crosses Wayne's mind to try to get away), then picks him up in the same fashion, walks to the back of the house, then throws him up onto the roof. Wayne scrambles quickly to make sure he doesn't fall off his perch.

Aunt Rebecca says to Dad, "Buck, why did you throw them up on the roof?"

Dad says, "Because they wouldn't stop fighting. I told them to stop."

Dad gets a great big grin on his face, waves to the boys (each on their own tower), then says,

"Look, they stopped."

Dad walks up to the barbecue grill and joins Uncle Gordo, who has been looking at Dad incredulously.

Uncle Gordo says, "Buck, we're going to be eating in a few minutes, don't you want to get the boys down?"

Dad turns and looks at Danny. Danny and Wayne have been sticking their tongues out at each other, so Danny doesn't immediately notice Dad.

Dad asks, "Danny, if I let you down to eat hotdogs, will you promise not to fight with Wayne?"

Danny doesn't answer right away, but turns and looks at Wayne, which is the wrong thing to do.

Dad spins back to the grill and announces to all, "Danny and Wayne have decided they like living on roofs, and don't feel like eating hotdogs."

Within a few minutes, both families are eating hamburgers, hotdogs, potato salad, and barbecue beans. Danny and Wayne are now sitting and watching the family eat. All of the family but Dad steal a glance at them during the meal. When Dad finishes, and it takes a long time for that to happen, he walks over the Danny, makes him promise he will not fight with Wayne for the rest of the night—which he does—then has him jump down into his outstretched arms. Dad whispers for Danny to go see his Mom at the picnic table for his dinner, and then walks over to go though the same steps with Wayne. Danny and Wayne pass by each other, but they don't even acknowledge the other. It's best they don't tempt fate. Besides, most of their anger left them while they were sitting on the roofs.

3

By October, Eddie is old enough to go out trick-or-treating with his older brothers. Danny dresses like Frankenstein, Wayne is a pirate, and Eddie is Casper the friendly ghost. Mom fixes an early dinner before they go out (which is her usual trick to try to get the boys to cut back on their candy eating—at least a little). Danny is upset that Wayne has a cool curved sword and that he decided on being Frankenstein instead of a pirate too. He runs into his bedroom, and searches for a weapon he can use, and finally settles on a baseball bat, which he thinks is appropriate. Dad doesn't and makes him put it back; explaining that Wayne's sword is a cheap plastic one, and the baseball bat is real; he could do real damage with that thing. Danny decides he will somehow make Wayne give him his sword before the night is over. The children are in their costumes, and the parents have their assignments: Dad will accompany all three boys at least around this block, and possibly two, depending on how Eddie is holding up. Mom will stay here with Lee, and hand out candy to the visiting trick-or-treaters. Danny and Wayne are bouncing with delight at the front door as they have had to wait through 364 days of "Un-Halloweens". They talk about how they hope they get their favorite candy. Any candy bar is tops, followed by pixie-sticks, wax lips, candy cigarettes, Tootsie rolls, sweet-tarts, lollipops, and gum. Other things, that unscrupulous adults may drop in their bags (which they most certainly don't like), are; popcorn balls or Rice Krispies bars wrapped in cellophane, any fruit, baggies full of popcorn or pretzels, and candy corn (usually tossed in loose, and eaten last if the boy isn't already sick from eating the better stuff). Oddly enough, the best part of the evening after the trick-or-treating, was "The trade". All of the boys who had any candy at all would retire to their bedroom to trade what they didn't like for what they did.

A typical trade might look something like this, "I'll give you five black licorice sticks for your Baby Ruth candy bar."

It was an effective way to improve your situation with your supply of candy. Nobody liked to be stuck with candy he isn't going to eat. Another entertaining thing that happened during the bartering was that all participants eat his own best candy as fast as he can, to take it off the table as a tradable item. In this way, trading candy was like playing poker; where the object was to get rid of all your bad cards. All of these thoughts (and more) are running through Danny and Wayne's minds as Dad finally opens the door. Dad holds the door open as Danny and Wayne file out across the porch and down the steps. Eddie moves out the door and on to the porch just as Mom tells Dad to be careful, drawing his attention just long enough for things to go wrong in a hurry. Once Eddie gets trundling across the porch, for reasons that are still not clear (although not being able to see through the Casper mask eyes is part of the problem), Eddie forgets about the porch steps in front of him, then walks off, is briefly airborne, and then falls on his face. Danny and Wayne had turned around to wait on their Dad (as their teaching dictated), so had a perfect vantage point to watch Eddie's flight, and were puzzled by what they saw; trying to make sense out of why he did at all. Everyone knows there are three steps down from the front porch. Eddie takes a few seconds to realize he just fell on his face and needs to be telling someone about it, so starts to scream from low-level first, gaining volume every second, like a teapot building to a whistle. Dad is out of the door immediately, across the porch in a single large stride, and on to the sidewalk with a leap off of the porch on to the sidewalk. He bends down to pick up Eddie and see what damage he had, giving Danny and Wayne a withering look. Eddie is now crying so loudly for so long he has trouble catching his breath and is doing so in gasps. As Dad picks Eddie up on to his feet, the mask has fallen down and is hanging from his neck. Blood is freely flowing from Eddie's nose, leaving a long stain on the white costume. Danny has the thought that after his Dad gets the flow of blood stanched, and they continue on their trick or treating journey, Eddie's costume will truly be scary with the added touch of real blood.

Mom runs out on to the porch with Lee in her arms, asking, "What happened?" as she negotiates the front steps and joins Dad.

He responds while glaring at Danny and Wayne, "I don't know, but they had something to do with this!"

Dad stands, picks Eddie up into his arms and carries him into the house, giving his most disapproving look to Danny and Wayne before going up the stairs to the porch. Mom follows behind with Lee.

As Dad goes through the front door, he yells over the continued screams from Eddie, "Halloween is over. Get your butt's in the house, now!"

Danny and Wayne don't argue, or try to explain to their Dad what happened—they know better. The children in this house have no voice, and Danny and Wayne know it is best if they keep theirs to themselves. They also know that they dare not go back to their bedroom, so they go into the house and just stand near where their Mom is currently helping Dad stem the flow of blood from Eddie's nose. They continue to stand while Mom strips Eddie out of his costume, and puts him into his pajamas. Eddie is now just sniffling, which is an enormous relief to everyone (nobody has ever questioned the exceptional lung capacity of that boy). Once Mom and Dad have put Eddie to bed, they both return, and the interrogation begins. Nothing can convince Dad otherwise, that Danny and/or Wayne pushed Eddie off of the porch; because they are mean and always do things like this. Danny is finally asked for his version of the story, but Dad isn't buying it. Dad sends Danny and Wayne to bed, and told to think about what they have done, and how they ruined Halloween for everyone. It isn't until the following day that Mom has a chance to talk with Eddie and discovers that he did—under his own direction—walk off the porch. Of course, it's too late to re-do

Halloween, and Dad will not apologize for jumping to conclusions. He says instead, that he was entirely justified in reacting the way he did, because what he imagined was what they would normally do; a no-win situation for the boys.

4

It is shortly after 10:30 AM on Friday November 22nd. Mom, who is out front with Lee in his stroller, has been leisurely pushing him along the sidewalk, stopping and chatting with friends who happen to be out. She is currently speaking to Barbara, who is two houses down, when a next-door neighbor rushes out into the yard.
She yells, "Oh My God, the president was just shot in Dallas!"
Barbara and Mom both cry out, "What?"
The size and importance of what they have just been told—like all such dreadful news; will take a while to make sense.
The woman, is now crying, and repeats, "President Kennedy has been shot; in Dallas."
Barbara runs to her house without saying another word. The deliverer of this unwelcome newsstands staring at Mom for a few more seconds, then spins and runs off into her house. Mom, thinking there must be some mistake, walks briskly with Lee, back to her own home. She gets inside the house, not even bothering to remove Lee from his stroller first and then turns on the TV. She doesn't bother to sit down, but watches as the announcers begin to lay out what happened. As some of the preliminary (and unconfirmed) reports begin to come in, she stands next to the sofa. She watches, as two Catholic Priests, hurry inside Parkland Hospital, to be by the president's side. When the official announcement of the president's death comes, Mom is motionless. She reacts to this announcement by starting to cry. Danny, who has chosen this moment to enter the living room, finds his Mom racked with sobs, and thinks someone close (Dad, Lee), must have just died.
Mom sees Danny and reaches out to him, saying, "The president is dead."

Danny doesn't know who she is talking about.

Mom continues, "President Kennedy. The president of the United States…just died."

Danny finally realizes who she is talking about; the nice man who has the pretty wife, and son with the name he likes (John-John). Now Danny understands why his Mom is crying, and now he feels some of the same loss she feels, so joins her in crying. They cry for a long time, and when Mom finally stops, so does Danny. Mom doesn't question Danny's sincerity, since there have been times when he has been able to express emotion (very seldom to be sure), and she welcome's these times gladly. Danny wanders back out into the backyard where Wayne has been playing to tell him about the president. Wayne knows John-John, so also remembers his daddy. There is no crying this time, but their mood is somber. On the radio from the kitchen, a song by Skeeter Davis can be heard playing, "The end of the World."

The Monster in the Light

It is now January of 1964. Wayne has just turned four, and Eddie, who is two years and eight months old, is now at prime hitting-age…but this poses some new problems. Danny and Wayne have to be careful hitting Eddie. Their Dad will never ask who started it, but will always side with Eddie. Danny has given this problem a lot of thought and decides that he will have to rule over Eddie with fear and intimidation. He tests the intimidation tactic first by telling Eddie that if he doesn't do what he tells him, he will get a beating. Unexpectedly, Eddie immediately tells their parents, and Dad punishes Danny, for the threat itself. Danny has a lively imagination, and he analyzes the tools at his disposal. After much thought, he knows that he can use his storytelling ability to inspire fear in his younger brother Eddie. That night, he decides to try this out. All three boys sleep in the same bedroom, with Danny and Wayne on the first bunk bed (Danny on top, and Wayne on the bottom), and Eddie on the bottom of the second bunk. Danny decides to make up a story, which he will impart to Wayne and Eddie when they go to bed tonight, and see if it proves to be a good weapon. That night, all three boys, are kneeling at Wayne's bed and saying their prayers, as their parents watch from the doorway.

They say in unison, "Now I lay me, down to sleep, I pray thee Lord, my soul to keep. If I should die before I wake, I pray thee Lord, my soul to take. God bless Mommy and Daddy, my brothers, my aunts, uncles, and cousins, Grandma and Grandpa, all my friends and all my enemies. Amen."

They get tucked in after All three boys jump into their beds. Mom walks over and kisses all three boys goodnight. Dad says his goodnight's from the doorway.

As soon as the door is closed, Danny begins to tell his story, "Do you guys know about the monster in the light?"

"What light?" Wayne asks.

"The one up there," Danny says while he points to the square, single-bulb ceiling light, in the center of the room.

A new TV show just started last month called, "Outer Limits", which his parent's, let him watch. He wonders why they let their kids watch the show because it is scary. Eddie is too young to watch it (and goes to bed early anyway), but Danny and Wayne are always paying rapt attention to every minute of the show.

"Do you remember on the Outer Limits show last week about the alien bugs with people faces, and they came to earth, and could climb walls?"

Wayne and Eddie remain silent. They are both staring at the light.

"They were misfits from another planet. A misfit is a monster. They can make a buzzing sound that hurts people; then they eat you."

Wayne and Eddie are remarkably still.

"One of those misfits is living in our light. The monster is my friend, and he will attack you if you try to follow me when I leave this bedroom. It will come out of the light and drop on you and eat you. It will buzz, and you will never be able to run. You will freeze while it eats you."

Danny drops to the floor from the upper bunk (which causes both Wayne and Eddie to let out spontaneous yells of surprise), and walks to the door. He opens the door a few inches and looks out to see if Mom or Dad is awake. He can hear Dad's voice from their bedroom, so goes through the door quickly to the living room, then turns around to wait. He stands against the wall in the shadows for the next fifteen minutes and never sees his bedroom door open. It looks as if his plan has worked, and he is tremendously excited about it.

Danny goes into the bathroom, to pee, and thinks, "If his Mom or Dad catch him out of bed; he will have a good excuse."

When Danny gets back to his room and opens the door, there is just enough light for him to see that both of his brothers are still staring at the light. He doesn't try to lessen the impact of having a monster in the light, so his brothers will be able to sleep. Remember that Danny is a bigger monster than this creation of his imagination. Danny smiles as he jumps up on to his bed, and as is always the case, climbs under the covers, takes a few deep breaths, then fades off into sleep. We are standing in the middle of the room and can barely hear Danny snoring. Wayne is still staring at the light, afraid to move, for fear of the monster dropping down and getting him. Eddie is also staring, but starts to blink from sleep starting to overwhelm him. We watch as his eyes close for longer each time, until they finally close and don't open again. We are pleased that at least this brother was able to escape his brother's story-fabricated monster. Wayne, however, is another matter. For an extraordinarily long time, his eyes continue to stare. After more than an hour, Wayne's eyes start to blink too, and finally sleep claims him.

The next day (early as usual), all of the boys come fully awake (as little children are wont to do), and walk across the room with Wayne and Eddie pausing to look at the light above them. Maybe they think they dreamt the monster. Maybe they think that Danny made everything up. He is so convincing; they can never be sure. By the time, they have crossed the hallway and have entered the family room—Danny detoured to the TV to turn it on—and flop on the couch, to watch their regular shows. It is obvious that the storytelling from the previous night has had an impact on Wayne and Eddie; they are truly subdued. They all sit in silence with no arguing or fighting…which is highly unusual. An hour later, they finally hear their parents in the hallway.

A few minutes later Dad walks in and sits down to talk, "Are you guys feeling alright? You sure have been quiet this morning, compared to your usual selves."

All boys look at their Dad, and as usual Danny speaks for all, "We're just hungry Dad."

Danny is already adept at re-directing attention on to other subjects, and he knows of his Dad's fondness for food, so uses this food-card whenever he can.

Dad, loving food more than most, immediately feels his Son's pain and acts on it, by yelling towards the kitchen, "Jean? Do you have breakfast started?"

Mom yells from the kitchen, "Yes!"

Satisfied he has kept his Sons from starving, Dad reaches over and pats Danny's leg lovingly, then stands and walks to the entrance of the living room.

He turns and says, "Hold on troops. Chow will be on at."

He looks at his watch, and says, "oh-nine-hundred

All of the boys laugh because they love it when their Dad plays army. They know their Dad was once in the army, so they know this is real. They have no idea what "oh-nine-hundred" means, but they hope it is soon, because they are hungry. Dad gives them all his biggest smile, then leaves. A half hour later Dad yells to the boys that breakfast is ready. The boys all run to the table, sitting in their assigned seats. Mom carries a large plate with bacon and sausage and sets it near Dad. She goes back into the kitchen and quickly returns with another big platter stacked with pancakes.

The boys all shout out together, "Pancakes!"

Mom makes one more trip to the kitchen returning with syrup and butter.

Dad asks, "Where are the eggs?"

"I figured with the meat and pancakes, we didn't need eggs."

"You figured wrong."

The boys are listening to this little volley hoping that this fight will not escalate and ruin breakfast, but look down at their plates as if they aren't paying attention.

Eddie suddenly says, "I want fring fries."

This is the way Wayne says "French fries", and Eddie is trying to imitate him. Dad, who has just taken a sip of his orange juice while still glaring at Mom, laughs out loud, dribbling the juice down his shirt. Danny and Wayne are laughing too at this unexpected dilly. This unexpected humor catches Mom off guard as she is lost in thought trying to come up with a retort back to Buck, and she starts to laugh too. Eddie is the only one not laughing, but is instead, looking from face to face with an amused look. He knows he is the one who said "the funny", but has no idea what it was that was funny.

Not deterred, Eddie adds, "How about sketty! Mmmmmm."

The others howl louder. This one is another attempted imitation of Wayne trying to say spaghetti. Eddie, wanting to be a part of this fun starts to laugh too. It is a while before the laughing starts to settle down. Like all natural laughter, it has totally diffused the earlier tension between Mom and Dad. Mom and Dad serve breakfast to the kids, and all are eating with a vigor made possible by the laughter. After a few minutes, as the eating slows from its initial frenzy,

Danny takes a drink of his orange juice, swallows it down, then turns to Eddie and says condescendingly and good-naturedly, "Fring fries!"

This starts all the children laughing all again, but Mom and Dad just look on amused. Eddie loves his new role as an entertainer, and looks forward to his new position; f only he knew what he said that was so funny. Dad and the boys all eat much more than Mom would have thought possible. The amount of food Buck and the three boys just ate, would have fed twice as many people in her family when she was growing up. This is one of the many realities she has had to face in being a Walker. The grocery bill has been double what she would have expected; and just wait until Eddie and Lee is Danny and Wayne's age and they all eat like this.

Dad says, "After breakfast, I have some work to do. After that, how about we all walk to the Circle K and get some ice cream?"

Cheers all around from the boys since they will get to pass by Green Valley and the witches house, then ice cream. That's a pretty enjoyable day all around.

Two hours later, the family of six is now walking out to the front sidewalk. Danny and Wayne are in the lead, Mom is following just behind holding Eddie's hand, and Dad is following at the back pushing the stroller with Lee aboard.

Danny and Wayne speed ahead and stay at the curb, looking both ways for traffic, then announcing in stereo, "All clear!"

The family crosses this familiar section of road, and as is the case every time they take this journey, Danny and Wayne…and now Eddie, stop to marvel at the number 57 and arrow on the sidewalk. The number and arrow fade a little more each day, but this fact does not diminish the impact it has on these adventurous young children. The Pine tree is still there too; taller every time they see it, it seems. The boys have started craning their necks to look at the top in wondrous awe, and wonder where the treasure is; buried underneath, or tied to a branch above. Once again, they reach Green Valley, and now there are three Walker boys running crazily through the hedges. Dad has given Danny and Wayne, the responsibility to keep an eye on Eddie, so he doesn't get lost down a dead-end. Danny and Wayne nod, but forget this promise the second they have left this world, and entered the next. After far too short a time, the trains whistle blows, and two-thirds of the boys emerge from the hedge. Eddie is missing, and without hesitation, Danny returns to the maze, this time on a different mission. When Danny hasn't found him after a while, he decides to check on all of the other exits. Sure enough, Eddie has gotten turned around, and has exited on the opposite side of Green Valley. Danny grabs the hand of his crying little brother, and decides not to go through the hedges because it will take too long. Instead, they walk along the edge to the parking lot. Mom and Dad are visibly relieved, as Mom takes the hand of Eddie, then off to their next destination they go. As they come to the Witches house, the dark sedan that is usually parked there is missing. This should reduce the boy's fear somewhat, but it doesn't. Danny is unnerved because he can't imagine creatures of the night out during the day. If this is true, and it looks as if it is, this is a whole new ballgame. Now, they aren't safe, even during the day.

A terrible idea seizes Danny, "What if the Witch, or the Vampire, or the various monsters that live there were hiding along the trails of Green Valley? It's right across the street from there. Why hadn't he seen this before?"

This theory is so powerful Danny catches his breath. Mom and Dad stand a long way away, whenever he and his brothers are running the trails. Far enough away, anyways, for a Witch to put a spell on them, or a Vampire to make them into new Vampires, or monsters to do things to them he can't even imagine. What if they just catch them and bring them back in the witch's house? They would never escape from there; if they lived past the first night that is. Danny forces himself to look away and runs after his Mom and Dad, who are twenty feet ahead. By the time the family is at the end of the block, the house has almost been forgotten—just a small tickle in his subconscious mind. As they stand on the corner of Grant and Mount Vernon, the "Other" Green Valley is on their right. This one is only half the size of "Their Green Valley," and is right up against the far busier four-lane Mt. Vernon highway. For quite a while now, all of the boys have been begging their parents to let them go running in this other magical place. Mom and Dad have been opposed because not only is it right next to the highway, it also has a downward slope on the highway side. They both expect one of the boys, running with a full head of steam, flying down a trail, unable to stop, and right out into the road. Dad turns to look at his boys, waiting for the matter to come up, and sure enough they don't disappoint.

Wayne says, "If we walk slowly, can we go in?"

Eddie says, "I'll hold a hand."

Danny is uncharacteristically quiet on the subject and looks away when his dad glances his way.

Dad's eyebrows go up in surprise, and he favors a look to Mom that says, "What's up with him?"

Dad pushes the cross walk button and looks at Danny again. This just isn't like him at all; to not argue for a jaunt into the second green valley. They cross the highway with the green, and turn left. They all come to the Circle K, get their ice cream's, then sit out on the curb in front, like they always do. Danny, Wayne, and Eddie are sitting off to the side, trying to prove their independence, and their parents think it's cute. The cars and trucks, and large trucks speed by just fifty feet away, causing it to be noisy.

Danny is staring off at the traffic like the rest of the family, but unlike the others, he is exceptionally busy speaking to his two younger brothers, "Do you believe me now that there is a misfit that lives in our bedroom light?"

Danny turns to look at his brothers sitting next to him, and can see their answers in their eyes.

He continues, "We should never go into the 'Other Green Valley.' There is a Boogie Man that lives there."

Danny has turned to look at his brothers again and sees them whip their heads towards him, and both have surprised looks on their faces. Danny is wondering just how well he can control his brothers. The monster in the light was easy, because that was at night. This one, he knows, will be more of a challenge.

Wayne says. "You always say you want to go in that green valley. Just like us."

Wayne is now giving Danny a look of suspicion, as he is starting to suspect that Danny is pulling a fast one. He is trying to figure out what game Danny is playing.

Danny continues, "Remember last night I left? I went to the Witches house, to see what I could see since we have never gone there at night."

This is a lie, and Danny knows he may have trouble selling this one. Wayne is trying to remember if Danny had been missing long enough to do that. Danny continues to sell his story and knows he may still lose his brothers on his version of the truth.

He says, "When I got to the witches house, I saw the Boogie Man leaving there. I think he was visiting. I followed him to the other green valley, where he went in and disappeared."

Wayne asks suspiciously, "What does he look like?"

Danny responds quickly, "He carries smoke around him, so he is hard to see, so he can sneak up on you. He is made of leaves and sticks, and mud, so you can't see him when he stops walking in the woods... or lies down."

Wayne's doubtful look softens a little, as he looks off at a passing motorcycle and takes a few more licks from his ice cream.

Eddie asks, "He has a house there?"

Wayne, with a skeptical look towards his younger brother, says, "Did you see a house?"

Danny jumps in, "He does have a house…under the ground. There is a hole in the ground that you fall into down to his house, then he eats you."

The story still sounds ridiculous to us (the witnesses), but we see the look on Wayne's face go from skeptical to understanding, then fear, all within a few seconds. Danny has set the hook, and now begins to reel in his catch. Eddie has been watching Wayne for his reaction, and when he sees Wayne finally believe, he gets seriously scared. Mom, who chooses this moment to glance towards the boys, has concern when she sees the frightened looks on her two youngest boy's faces.

She asks, "What's wrong with you guys?"

Danny. As usual, answers for them all, "I just told them a scary story about the Witches House, that's all."

"Is that what he just did?"

Wayne and Eddie nod in agreement.

Mom turns and looks at Danny and says, "You stop scaring your little brothers with that wild imagination of yours. Talk about fun things, not that stupid house. You're going to give your brothers nightmares."

"OK Mommy. I'm sorry," Danny says as he hugs his Mom and gives her his large and innocent smile.

Sometimes she can't help but love this kid, and all is well. As Danny is hugging his Mom, and she is rubbing his back, he looks over at his brothers, who are still staring at him with scared looks, and gives them a different smile altogether. This is his crocodile smile…the evil one we have seen before. A black 1960 Buick LeSabre pulls up and plays a few words of a song from "West Side Story" before the motor shuts off, "…Tonight, tonight, won't be just any night."

Touching the Moon

It is now past ten o'clock that night, and Danny and Wayne have been lying awake since their bedtime of eight o'clock. They are so excited they can't stand it, and have been waiting patiently for the deep vibration of their Dad's voice (sounding more like the deep rumble of an extremely large truck), through the wall to stop. This will mean that their parents have finally gone to sleep. Just after dinner tonight while Danny and Wayne had retired to their bedroom to play with Danny's Tinker Toy set (because there was a boring show on TV), their conversation turned to the large pine tree across the street (Not talking about the Witches house, thank you very much.) The old fascination of the marker on the sidewalk and the Pirate's treasure, have not left them. They still believe that the treasure is somewhere within its branches. It has to be. Maybe they will need to dig down through the pine needles, or there might be an opening in the tree. Both boys are discussing how tall the tree is when suddenly

Danny says, "I'll bet if we climb to the top of that tree. All the way to the top, we will be able to reach out and touch the moon."

The awesomeness of this idea sinks in for both boys.

Wayne says in a whisper, "What if the treasure is at the top too?"

"What are you whispering about?" Eddie asks.

Danny responds, "Nothing. This is none of your business. Go to sleep."

Eddie quiets but Danny knows he will have to handle him later. If he doesn't, Eddie can ruin him and Wayne's plans, because he can't climb trees. Soon, Danny and Wayne are whispering again, and the former joy overtakes them. Each possibility excites them all the more, their fast whispering speeds up and slows, and a then speed up and slows. They decide that they will climb to the top and if they come upon a treasure; even better. More than hearing their Dad's voice stop, they perceive the sudden quiet, which is unsettling. Both boys are already dressed; tennis shoes included.

Danny begins his story, "Eddie, the misfit is in the light again."

This implication that the misfit can go out and about adds another dimension of fear to Eddie that Danny did not intend. Up until this realization, Eddie thought that if he ran fast enough, the monster wouldn't get him. Now, with the understanding that the monster can come after him, wherever he goes, there is no way he is leaving his bed. Danny is prepared for a long session of convincing his brother, so is surprised at the simplicity of his task.

Danny says, "Me and Wayne are leaving. If you follow us...."

"I won't. I'll stay right here," responds Eddie.

Danny is surprised and doesn't trust their good fortune; but he has to be sure.

He continues, "If you tell Mom..."

"I won't tell Mommy or Daddy. I promise."

Danny is still not sure, and he needs to be, so says, "If you tell..."

"You'll beat me up."

Danny stares at Eddie in confusion; wondering if he is somehow pulling a fast one on him. After all, these things have rules, which are always followed the same way. Danny is finally satisfied, but doesn't know why his job was so easy. Without a word, he slips off of his bunk and walks over to Eddie's bed. He holds his fist in front of Eddie's eyes, and then opens his eyes wide. Eddie—knowing the appropriate response; nods his head in agreement. Wayne is already at the door waiting, so Danny quietly joins him, then they are out of the door, down the hall to the back door, then out—moving much too quietly for children this little. They go through the side gate and stop at the front edge of the side wall. A quick glance up and down the road to make sure nobody sees them, and then they stop short and lay down instinctively to hide. A 1955 Mercury Monterey in light-blue and yellow outline around the distinctive wood grain side panels (what their Dad calls a "Woody"), flies by in front of them. The song, "Fly me to the Moon" is blasting from the car as it moves down the street.

Once the brake-lights come on as the car stops at the end of the street off they go across the street and the grass on the other side of the street, then under the boughs of the giant pine to safety. Peeking out though the branches, they are happy to realize they can see out but can't be seen. They are able to test this hypothesis by Danny leaving the back of the tree and trying to see his brother, but can't. The next thing they are tremendously happy about is, all of the branches above them are needle and pine cone free; those sticky things, keeping to the ends of the branches only. Danny and Wayne are already accomplished tree climbers, and know that climbing this tree will be remarkably fast and easy. With no further hesitation, both boys begin to climb. We can see these boys climb trees regularly, because, within a few minutes, they are already over 50 feet up. A few minutes later, at seventy feet high, they come out of the protection of the tree's upper-most canopy and are now climbing in the open from branch to branch hanging from a trunk that has narrowed to just over a foot in diameter. Danny now stops, looking up to the top of the tree just ten feet above. Wayne, who has been climbing below Danny, now moves around to the other side, so he can climb up, to the same height. The moon is not directly above them, but a little towards their house, so they will have to reach to touch it.

"Wayne, once we get to the top I will reach out to touch the moon first, but you need to hold my belt to help hold me up, so I don't fall," says Danny.

Wayne nods, as they climb the last ten feet, not noticing or caring that the part they are now holding on to have been noticeably swaying, and that the branches they are now gripping, and the others they are standing on, have grown much thinner. They are at the top just a minute later. The view from the top of the tree is spectacular. The wind has picked up some, which is enough to push some of the smog away, giving them a view of the scattered lights of the city for five miles in every direction. At any other time, the boys may have sat and admired this breathtaking view, but they are on a mission that has given them laser focus.

Without hesitation, and with no fear whatsoever, Danny turns his back to the trunk, still reaching back with his left hand, and says, "Hold on to my belt."

Wayne says, "I am. Feel it?"

Danny nods and leans out; reaching high and far for the moon.

Wayne, who has a slightly different perspective on where Danny is, and where the moon is, says, "You're too far to the right. Move left."

Danny does, but soon gets frustrated for his lack of success.

"Let me try now," says Wayne, already starting to circle the tree to where Danny is.

Danny wants to try longer, but he made a promise to his brother. Danny circles to the other side, and grabs a hold of his brother's belt. Wayne reaches out, and Danny sees that he is reaching too far right, then suddenly a loud snap, and his brother is falling. We hear a single short "Ahhhh", and then Wayne is slowing down from Danny's grip on his belt. Danny tries to get a better grip on Wayne until his feet can get onto a branch when the branch under his feet snaps. Danny and Wayne are in free fall now, each on their own side of the tree. Danny still has control of Wayne's belt. They only fall five feet before Danny hooks his free arm over a branch which doesn't break. Wayne immediately grabs a branch with his hands and walks his feet onto a solid branch below. They are not as shook up as they should be, but it is enough for Danny and Wayne to understand the night is over, and it's time to climb down. They don't say anything on the climb down, because they are so disappointed. Once on the ground, they move with their heads down at a slower pace than when they first arrived. Danny is absently rubbing his arm, that he hooked, on the branch, to prevent the fall. We get the feeling that if someone catches them out here, given their current mood, they will not even care. Danny stops on the sidewalk in front of their house, and then looks up longingly at the moon. Wayne looks up too.

Danny starts to mumble something, which Wayne can't even hear, but we soon learn he is singing a song, "I see the moon; the moon sees me, down through the leaves of the old oak tree."

He stops as suddenly as he started. This is one of the songs the family sings when on long trips, to help pass the time. After a few seconds, Danny sighs in frustration, and then continues on to the back door. Both boys make it to their bedroom where they take off their clothes, and put on their pajamas, climbing into bed without a word to each other. Their hands are sticky from the sap, but they are too tired to wash their hands.

They lie still for several minutes when out of the darkness, Danny says, "The moon wasn't big enough. That's why we couldn't touch it."

From Eddie, who they thought was asleep, "The moon?"

Nothing else is said for another minute.

Then Danny adds, "The closer the moon is, the bigger it is. Like a ball."

Eddie says, "What ball?"

Wayne is listening closely and is not as depressed as before. Danny is now sitting up in bed as the earlier disappointment is turning back into hope.

Danny says, "We can watch for the big moon, and then try again."

"Yes. That will be nice. You almost touched the moon!" Wayne says.

Danny turns to his brother, and they can barely see each other in the dark, but it is enough, and says, "You almost touched the moon too!"

Eddie cries, "I want to touch the moon," not having any idea what they are talking about.

Danny lies back down, and both boys are asleep within minutes. Danny and Wayne have the same smiles on their faces, no doubt dreaming about what they will do after they touch the moon. What will it feel like? Eddie decides he will ask his older brothers about the moon (or the ball); they were talking about, tomorrow morning. Within a few seconds, he too drifts off to sleep.

Wanderings

It is a beautiful bright and cooler than normal early morning in June of 1964, and Danny is on the move. We are following him as he now walks north down the alley towards Hazel Avenue. Danny almost always moves quickly, as if always on a mission. He passes kids on bikes and tricycles, and adults hand watering bushes, and washing their cars. He barely draws attention from anyone, as if he is somehow partly invisible; he is wearing jeans and a red t-shirt instead of his usual subdued colors, so he isn't quite camouflaged. Danny now crosses Hazel and turns left down Bunker Hill drive. He reaches the fifth house on the left, and we can see a girl about Danny's age sitting on the stoop. She has long flowing blond hair, and large sapphire-blue eyes. She is wearing jeans and has on a white blouse, and brown sandals. She waves at Danny and a smile that has so much energy, so much life-affirming beauty spreads across her face; touching her eyes and making them shine. She holds out her hand to him as he nears the stoop. He takes her hand then sits down next to her. To the side of the porch, we see a curtain part, and a woman—an older version of this young beauty on the porch—looks on, and gives her version of her daughter's smile. The curtain closes.

"I'm glad you're here, Danny," says the girl.

"Hi Emma; I told you I was coming over," responds Danny, a little defensively.

"I like it when you're here."

"OK."

The door behind them opens, and Emma's Mom walks out on the stoop. Danny and Emma have both turned and look up at her.

"Hi Danny, how are you Hon?" asks Emma's Mom.

"Good," a quiet and subdued response from Danny.

We can see a camera in Emma's Mom's hands.

"I'm going to take a picture of you two. I've been meaning to do this for a while now, but I keep forgetting."

She moves past Danny and Emma and takes up a position five feet in front of them on the sidewalk.

"Say cheese!"

Both say cheese as they give their biggest smiles. Emma's Mom has them smile again as she takes a second picture. As Emma's Mom walks back up on the porch, she lays her hand gently on Danny's shoulder.

As he looks up at her, she asks, "Would you like to come in for breakfast Danny?"

"No thank you. I'm not hungry."

"OK. Let me know if you change your mind."

Emma's Mom goes back into the house; looking back once more before closing the door. Danny and Emma are both staring off at the houses and trees across the street. A bright-red cardinal is now dancing from branch to branch, on a Crape Myrtle with white flowers. The petals are drifting in a mini-snow-storm lazily to the lawn and the street below. A few of the petals sail like tiny ships down the small river in the gutter. Danny follows the river upstream with his eyes to find the source, and sees a man at the end of the block washing his 1959 Tin Red Buick Convertible.

"I can't wait until first grade starts," says Emma.

"I don't want to go."

Emma turns and looks at Danny closely as he turns back to watch the cardinal.

"You don't want to be stuck in school, because you like to do what you want."

"Yeah. That's it."

"You like to play in sprinklers, and go to friend's houses when you want."

"Yeah."

"My next door neighbor, Sally, is going into second grade. She said all her friends are there at school. And that in her class, they had some worms that made silk. She said that, in first grade, they don't make you take naps."

"I don't know what silk is, and I have all the friends I need. Take naps? I never took naps in Kindergarten. Only babies take naps."

Danny shakes his head as if very disappointed by the nap thing. We know better. We have been following Danny for years now, and know that he will lie down and take a nap, whenever (and wherever) exhaustion overtakes him. Once, he was riding his tricycle in the driveway across the street (back when there were houses there, and before the college bought the homes and had them torn down), got tired, then just fell off his "trike", and went to sleep where he fell. Several minutes later, the dead boy, with tricycle nearby, was found by the man who owned the house, after coming home from work. In his mind, it looked as if the boy was shot off his bike. He left his car idling in the road and ran to the boy, expecting the worse. He was extremely happy—and extremely puzzled—to find Danny unharmed, but sleepy. He helped him back to his house, and even managed to get the tricycle to the yard too.

"Maybe we'll be in the same class this year, and get to sit next to each other." Emma says quietly and squeezes Danny's hand.

Danny turns and looks at Emma, but now she is staring off at a woman pushing a white stroller. The woman is wearing a white dress and white shoes. A white pill-box hat (which looks like the hatbox it came in), sits at an angle on top of her head. Danny sees Emma smile at something she sees, so he turns and watches the woman.

"I don't like white," he says, rather strangely.

"I do. She's beautiful. I want a white dress and white hat someday; maybe when I get married."

"Married? Yuck, I'm never getting married."

"I think most people get married. I want white flowers for my bouquet. My Mommy had a white flower bouquet when she married my Daddy. They are beautiful. Like those white flowers on that tree," Emma says as she looks at the Crape Myrtle.

"I don't know what a "boo-kay" is, but it sounds silly to me."

Emma turns and smiles at Danny, somehow able to see through his little-boy-bluster, and see the real person underneath.

Danny, feeling uncomfortable by the closeness between him and Emma suddenly, says, "Well, I have to go to Richie's for breakfast."

Danny stands up quickly, not realizing he had just told Emma's Mom he wasn't hungry.

"We have food. Mama says you can eat with us," Emma says softly, with sadness in her eyes.

Danny is staring off down the block now as if he is already gone. Danny is decidedly distracted by his need to go, and Emma trying to get him to stay.

Danny turns back to her, "What?"

Before he gets a response, Danny gives her an enormous grin, waves, then walks away, looking once over his shoulder, and saying what his Dad always says,

"...After a while Crocodile"

Emma waves after Danny, and says, "See you later Danny."

Her smile slowly melts into a frown.

A 1950 candy-apple-red Buick Sedan cruises by, "The Wanderer," by Dion is playing, which drowns out Danny's ability to hear Emma's last statement.

Danny walks back the way he came, not bothering to look back. Emma continues to stare after him, and barely notices her Mom coming back out on the porch, sitting down next to her, and putting her arm around her.

Danny travels two blocks, taking a shortcut through an alley towards the end of his journey. Danny has been traveling erratically; running from house to house and slowing to look between the houses towards the front, carefully. He is acting as if the fear of running into something or someone frightens him. At the end of the alley, Danny runs around the side of the house on his left, then up on the porch, and without knocking, walks through the door. As we have seen before with Danny and all of his friends, nobody knocks. Richie and his family are already seated around the breakfast table as Danny heads their way.

"Hello Michael," says Richie's Mom (Betty Garrett).

Only certain people call Danny, Michael (His Mom and Grandma are two), and with these few, it's OK.

"Hey Danny," says Steve, Richie's oldest brother, roughing up the little hair on Danny's head while he says it.

Danny plops into his chair (or, it may as well be his, as much as he is here).

"Cheerios and toast?" asks Betty, as she stands, and moves, around the table, to give Danny the cereal, toast, and everything else he needs.

"How are your Mom and Dad doing?" she asks.

Danny mumbles through a mouth full of cereal, "They're doing OK."

"Your Mom is a righteous babe, Dude," Steve adds, while raising his eyebrows in exaggeration.

"Steven! You don't talk about adults that way. I don't even like you talking that way about girls your own age," Betty says with mixed indignation and (oddly enough), admiration.

Danny doesn't know what Steve is talking about concerning his Mom and doesn't care. He is truly focused on the toast now, which has real butter, and boysenberry jam; which is his favorite. Richie has finished with his breakfast and is now patiently watching Danny finish his.

"I have something I want to show you," Richie says.

Danny just stares at him, knowing that Richie doesn't need to be prompted to continue.

"Remember how we always look for gold and diamonds?"

"Oh brother! Here, we go with this crap again," Steve says as he gets up quickly from his seat, while shaking his head as he stares at Richie, and walks into the other room.

"Steven!"

"Sorry Mom."

Danny can hear Steve plop on the couch in the other room where cartoons can be heard. Danny recognizes the voices of Bugs Bunny and Daffy Duck. He doesn't care for either of these characters. He likes Elmer Fudd, Yosemite Sam, and his favorite; The Tasmanian Devil.

Richie continues, "I found something better than gold or diamonds."

Danny asks disapprovingly, "Not your Lite-Brite again?"

In the past, Richie has vastly enjoyed this game and has gotten way too excited (in Danny's opinion); at the different designs he has created on the board. Danny thinks the game is OK, but much prefers the guns and arrow toys.

"No, not my Lite-Brite," he says with a little anger in his voice.

He continues, "What I found is outside in the bushes. Come on."

Danny says, "*They're* out there, so I'm staying inside."

"Who's out there? Who are you talking about?" Betty asks while she stacks dishes in the sink.

Danny gives Richie an angry look, and responds, "The big kids."

"They won't bother you. Steven!" shouts Richie's Mom.

Steve walks back into the kitchen, "What? I was watching something."

"Keep an eye on your brother and Michael, when they go out front to play. OK? It seems the 'big kids' have been bothering them." Richie's Mom says and gives Steve a secret wink.

"Sure, come on little guys. Let's go outside on an adventure, and I'll beat up the big kids."

Danny doesn't fully understand sarcasm yet, but he is picking up the insincerity in Steve's voice. He wonders what this means. Steve leads them to the door then all three go out on the porch. Richie, excited with what he is about to show Danny runs to the end of the hedges that run along the front of their house. Danny doesn't follow right away, but is busy scanning the yards and sidewalks up and down the streets. When he doesn't see anyone, he is satisfied, so follows after Richie. At the top of the hedge, is a small bird's nest, filled with four small, multicolored pastel eggs.

Richie has a wide grin on his face and is saying, "You see? My

Mommy has things like this she calls jewels. It's better than gold and diamonds, right?"

"These are bird eggs. They have a Mama bird that sits on these," Danny says.

Richie is shaking his head and says, "No, no, no, these are jewels and they're mine."

He reaches into the nest and scoops up all the pastel colored speckled eggs into his palm. He is staring down at the eggs with such admiration; you would think the eggs are platinum.

"You better put those back. People aren't to touch eggs," Danny says.

Instead, Richie pushes the eggs into the front pocket of his jeans then looks up with an almost-wicked smile, and says, "I'm rich now. I can buy whatever I want at the store."

"Hey, watcha got there? You're rich, huh?" This voice is older and stronger.

Both boys turn around and five teenagers (three guys and two girls) confront them. These are the same kids, who have been terrorizing Danny over the past few months, causing him to sneak around this neighborhood, trying to avoid them. Danny and Richie both turn towards the porch where Steve should be standing, but he isn't there.

"I asked you a question Candyass. What did you just put in your pocket? You got money in there?" the largest of the teenagers asks Richie.

This leader is just shy of six feet tall, has black hair, and dark eyes (which are particularly, mean looking, because he doesn't blink and stares at the boys a long time, making you look away). His hair has just enough grease to keep it combed back, all day, and keep his bangs flipped up in James Dean style. A pack of cigarettes rolls up in his right t-shirt sleeve, as is the style with "tough guys" of the day.

The five teenagers now move to surround both boys. All five have the same predator smiles. They all have the same dark hair and either dark brown or black eyes. The two other guys have their hair slicked back like their leader. All wear white t-shirts, jeans with the pants legs rolled up and tennis shoes. The girls are both wearing jeans in the same rolled-up manner as the boys and white sneakers, but have black blouses instead of t-shirts. Danny had briefly wondered whether the girls would protect him and Richie, but now sees there isn't any chance of that (The girls look meaner than the guys). Danny glances at Richie wondering what he will say and sees he is crying and looking down at the ground.

"Ahhhh, look at the crybaby. Baby needs a bottle?" asks the leader.

"Maybe he needs his diaper changed," adds one of the girls.

There is laughter from all of them. Danny glances at the windows and door of Richie's house just a few feet away and wonders if he were to scream for help, would Richie's Mom or Steve come out here in time to save them? He decides they wouldn't.

The leader says, more seriously, "If you don't answer me now, punk, I am going to pound you, then take what you got in your pocket."

With no warning at all Richie runs between the girl on the left and the bushes; her grab coming up short, as he barely gets through.

"Hey you little son of a bitch!" yells the leader, as all five teenagers go after Richie.

Danny wonders how Richie thinks he can outrun these teenagers who have legs twice as long as his, but doesn't have to wonder long. Richie gets behind his family's 1957 black Bel-Air station wagon parked in the driveway, and instantly drops down and scrambles underneath. Danny has been standing watching this action like a spectator until he notices one of the girls has just remembered him and is coming back towards him.

"Come here Cutie. Sandra wants to see you."

She has the same strange smile, which makes Danny feel as if he is this girl's dinner. Danny doesn't yet know about people who speak in 3rd person about themselves, so thinks this girl is speaking about the other girl. He does know, however, that there is no way he can make it to the front door, or outrun any of these kids, so decides to join Richie under the car. He fakes left, and when the girl leans that way, he runs around her on the right, and drops to the ground at the back of the car, quickly scurrying underneath next to Richie. The boys don't talk to each other but watch the feet of their pursuers.

Danny sees the feet of the girl come up to join the others and hears, "It's not my fault. Little bastard faked me out. "

"That's OK. We'll get them out of there. Sergio, go find a stick."

An arm suddenly grabs Danny's ankle and starts to pull. Danny kicks his feet and gets free.

The teenager yells, "Ouch! That little dork kicked me!"

Now many arms are reaching under the car, trying to grab any limb they can. Danny and Richie are scrambling just out of reach for several seconds but suddenly they grab Danny's ankles with their hands, drag him out, and set him on the ground in their midst. Danny is surprised to see that Richie is already standing there, held by a guy and a girl. Danny has his arms pinned back by the large leader.

The leader says, "You made us work for this, so we are really going to enjoy pounding you now."

Richie is staring down at his pants in terror, totally oblivious to what is going on. A sound starts to escape from his mouth; a high-pitched keening, "No, no, no, Noooooo!"

The teenagers look at his pants, and several say at once, "He pissed his pants."

Now they are all laughing again.

The leader adds, "I don't want whatever was in that pocket now!"

Again there is laughter.

Without knowing why he does so, Danny speaks up and says, "They're eggs. Robin's eggs, I think."

The leader says, "Holy crap kid, are you a retard? Sticking eggs in your pocket?"

This is again followed by laughter.

"One punch each, for making us work getting at you," says the leader.

One of the guys goes to Richie and without any warning, punches him in the stomach. Richie yells out and grabs his stomach and falls to his knees (the broken eggs momentarily forgotten).

The leader says while looking at Danny, "Here, hold onto this one. I want to hit him, I don't like the way he looks at me."

After trading positions with two of the other guys, and without any warning, the kid hits Danny in the stomach causing him to yell out, and drop to the grass while holding his stomach.

A warning is now given to Danny to add insult to injury, "If I ever see your ass around here again, I'll beat you, within an inch of your life." The leader says.

Neither Danny nor Richie nod or say anything. Again, no response is required. As suddenly as they arrived, the teenagers walk away down the street. Several of them turn to look back and wave at the still prostrate boys, smiling as they do so. This whole episode played out in five minutes. During those five minutes, two cars drove by, and the drivers; one older man and one younger woman, did not want to get involved so kept on driving. Jody Jones, a new mother pushing her new baby girl in her carriage, had just turned the corner, intending to walk down this sidewalk. She saw the older kids—obviously some gang—circling some kids, and decided the safety of her child was more important, so turned around and decided to take a longer walk. Three housewives, including two mothers of two of the teenagers, have watched the action through their house windows, shaking their heads, and even getting moist eyes, but in the end; doing nothing. After a few minutes, the pain in his stomach subsides enough for Danny to stand and stumble to the front door of Richie's house. Just as, he is ready to knock on the door, to get help from within, he glances down the street and sees all of the teenagers frozen in place, and staring back at him. He knows this is a challenge. Richie, on his knees, is also looking down the street, then turns to Danny and shakes his head no. Danny understands this message so lowers his hand then walks off the porch on the other side, and disappears around the corner.

Danny is now walking back down the same alley he arrived, and is still anxiously watching for the teenagers. Maybe they want to have some fun with him again. Danny decides to head home. He doesn't feel like going anywhere else. He is walking much more slowly now, and unlike the usual bold confidence Danny exudes, he is now looking at the sidewalk in front of him, with head down and shoulders slumped. A man stands watering his bushes. He is wearing Bermuda shorts, Hawaiian shirt, white socks, and black work shoes.

He waves at Danny (who is visible now) and says, "Hey Kid! Are you alright?"

Danny continues on without acknowledging the man.

"Cat got your tongue?"

Danny has never understood this phrase but is particularly glad they don't own a cat. Danny is finally out of range of the prying stranger (thank God), and resumes being alone with his thoughts. If a person were to get a response from Danny on what is troubling him so much, he would probably be hard pressed to put it into any words. He stops at the corner of Hazel and Bunker Hill and looks down the street towards Emma's house. For a moment, he thinks that maybe he will go there and see her. In the end, he sighs and shakes his head. He doesn't feel like talking about what just happened, and he knows that Emma (as perceptive as she is), will know something is wrong. He continues home. He walks down his alley, through his back gate, then across the yard, and into his house. His Mom is in the laundry room, and rubs his head as he walks by. She doesn't ask him where he's been. A part of her doesn't want to know, or she will worry. Danny will be six in August, which she thinks is pretty old for him; but she knows that most people would consider him still a young child. The double-standard surprises her. She knows she would never be able to explain these thoughts to anyone, so decides to not try. Danny walks into the living room where he finds Wayne and Eddie on the couch watching cartoons, and Lee asleep in his crib. Danny grabs Eddie, not too kindly, and shoves him towards the middle of the couch before he flops down in his spot. The prime sitting spots are always on the end. This rule applies to sofas and car seats; the older the brother, the better the seat. Eddie protests briefly but is hardly interrupted from his focus on the show, "The Cisco Kid". Danny settles into "zombie-mode," where they watch whatever happens to come on TV. The show is at its end, where Pancho and Cisco laugh, while saying their famous lines.

Cisco says to Pancho, "Oh, Pancho!"

Then Pancho replies, "Oh, Cisco!"

Wayne and Eddie laugh hard and long as usual during this part, and turn and look at Danny, wondering why he is so quiet, and not laughing along. Danny is so serious looking, their curiosity is not enough for them to ask him, and they turn back to watch TV. A commercial comes on about a local community outreach program. The background music is, "Look for the Silver Lining."

Early Departure

It is a week later, and like most things with children, Danny has forgotten about his awful experience with the teenagers. In place of that incident in his memories is a lack of any interest in going to Richie's house again…ever. Forgotten, is the warning from the teenagers, but his mind has erected this "false-barrier", to protect him from further embarrassment and hurt. Danny is once again traveling with invisibility (his dark t-shirt is insufficient to explain this). A man trimming his tree doesn't even notice him as he walks by. Danny has his old confidence back, and his bearing and gait reflect this. He decides to go to Emma's today. He thinks he will have breakfast with her this morning, and an enormous smile blooms on his face as his pace quickens. Danny rounds the corner and starts down Emma's street. On the opposite side of the street an old woman pushes a black carriage. She is wearing black and dark grey clothes. Danny's shadow—which, just a few minutes before, had been stretching out before him, is now gone as a large storm cloud covers the sun. Danny's pace slows as he sees that Emma is not sitting on her stoop. She is almost always sitting on her stoop when he comes. He glances to his right expecting to see the bright red car, but in this strange darkening light, it looks darker—almost grey. He glances up ahead, expecting to see the beautiful Crape Myrtle with its white flowers (and the red cardinal if he is lucky), and seeing that all of the branches on the tree are trimmed off, shocks him. Danny has slowed his walk even more as he walks up Emma's sidewalk. He knocks on the screen door and waits. After half a minute, he knocks again. He starts to reach for the doorbell, when he hears the door opening. An old woman Danny does not know stands there on the other side of the screen staring at him. The stare lasts for just a few seconds before the old woman bursts into tears, and she thrusts the screen door open. Danny steps back in surprise, as the old woman's face, arranges itself into that of Emma's Mom. This face is not wearing make-up, the hair is tangled and greasy, and the eyes are swelled with deep-set dark rings. She has the haunted appearance of a mental patient…long forgotten, and no longer a part of this world. She is wearing jeans, and a too-large t-shirt (her ex-husband's), and is barefoot. While Danny is still trying to make sense of what he is seeing, Emma's Mom bends over and pulls Danny to her, hugging him fiercely and crying in great wrenching sobs. Danny does not hug her back. In fact, he has never quite known what to do with his hands when being hugged. He does, however, have an enormous lump in his throat, and is truly distressed at what is coming. Danny wants nothing more than for Emma's Mom to let him go, so he can get away from here as fast, and as far as he can. Because Danny knows that he wouldn't be able to speak if he had to he says nothing. Emma's Mom pulls away from him and looks at Danny with the saddest, most haunted eyes he has ever seen, and he decides he never wants to see eyes like this again.

She says, "Danny, you have always been a very good friend to Emma. I want to tell you how much I appreciate that…for always being there for…her."

She doesn't even bother wiping away the tears that are now freely streaming down her face. The intensity of her stare mesmerizes Danny, as her emotions continue to rack her whole body. Her crystal blue eyes are too beautiful and too terrible at the same time as they swallow him into their depths. It is way too much for him. He has to get away from here…from her. He must get away …

"Danny, Baby…several days ago, Emma went away."

The confused look on Danny's face tells her he doesn't understand. Why would Emma going away cause her Mom to cry like this?

She tries again, "Honey, Emma died."

Renewed tears stream down her face as she continues to lock eyes with Danny. For his part, Danny is not crying. He feels a profound emptiness like a part of him has been suddenly ripped away—some vital organ he needs to survive. Danny needs to get away from Emma's Mom more than ever now. She is now holding his hands at arm's length, and her intense (and needy) gaze hasn't faltered. Danny feels so overwhelmed with "something" he can't quite identify, he lets out a moan, that grows in loudness, every second, as he twists away from Emma's Mom, and runs as fast as he can across her yard and down the sidewalk.

In the furthest reaches of his hearing, he can barely make out, "Please don't go...," said in the saddest, most distressing way he has ever heard.

He doesn't dare go back; and fights the urge to look back. Danny is so dazed now; he isn't noticing any of the trees, houses, or people he passes. All people see him, and their hearts go out to this lost child. Some inquire after him, but he is moving too fast. These people have the overwhelming feeling that something of immense importance is lost forever; something that will never be again. Danny crosses the street and eventually slows to a walk, just as the skies open up in a great deluge. A black 1959 GMC 100 pickup crawls slowly by, and the driver side crank-out window is open enough for Danny to hear The Kingston Trio singing,

"Where have all the young girls gone?

Long time passing

Where have all the young girls gone?

Long time ago..."

Danny recalls another verse from this song, where it says,

"Where have all the flowers gone?"

This reminds him of Emma's statement about wanting a white bouquet of flowers, during her wedding.

Then, the last verse barges unbidden into his mind,

"Where have all the graveyards gone…"

Danny doesn't seem to notice the deluge as he stops on the sidewalk. His Dad has this album and song, and he has always loved it…until now. Now, this song has much more meaning. For the first time in Danny's short life, a song is speaking to him. Danny stands on the sidewalk, in this great downpour, and he cries for Emma, and her forfeited future. He cries for Emma's Mom too, but most of all he cries for the white wedding dress she would have someday worn. He misses her terribly already. He cries until he has no more tears and feels nothing else. Danny starts walking again, and as he approaches his alley's turnoff he suddenly freezes from what he sees on the corner in the distance; a crape myrtle with white flowers glows with supernatural light in the storm. Each delicate flower shines like lit from within. The branches and trunk shine as if glimmering jewels cover it, and reflect the light from the flowers. The enchanted tree draws Danny towards it. Without a conscious decision to do so, Danny starts to walk towards it. He has an overwhelming desire to reach this tree (to be near it), and can't explain why. He is wondering if there will be a red cardinal, hiding in the branches once he gets close enough to see. While Danny walks towards the tree, the light goes out. He comes to a sudden halt, looking at where the bright tree was, and his memory of it is still so strong, he fully expects it to come back. After a few more seconds, Danny slowly nods his head as if to say, "Of course it went out," then turns and continues down the alley. The car, whose headlights had illuminated the tree just moments before, as it sat idling at the curb (perhaps waiting for the rain to subside), has turned off its headlights. Danny gets home and makes it to the bathroom without running into his Mom, for which he is hugely grateful. Danny is decidedly dazed and wants to be alone. He uses the hand towel to dry himself off, focusing on his head. In the bedroom, he strips out of all his sopping clothes and has just put on a dry pair of underwear when his Mom comes in.

She says, "There you are! When I heard the thunder, then the heavy rain, I was worried about you. Hold on a second."

Mom exits the room, and in a few moments, returns with a large bath towel that she uses to dry his still-wet body. Danny has started to shiver, so she helps him on with the rest of his clothes. During all of this, Danny has been remarkably quiet.

She feels his forehead, and then says, "Got stuck in the storm, huh? Are you feeling OK? Were you at Richie's?"

Danny nods three times (once for each question), continuing to stare off in an extraordinarily uncharacteristic way.

Mom feels his face again and says, "You feel a little clammy. Maybe you need to lie down for a while."

Danny nods again. In the end, she decides to change him into his pajamas, so he'll be more comfortable. After Mom covers Danny, he stares off into the odd almost-dark gloom which is always created when a large storm happens during the day. He does not cry. In fact, his mind isn't thinking much of anything at all right now. It's as if the part of his mind that makes connections; that helps people move, and think, and talk, is now gone. After a few minutes of staring at the unsympathetic shadows, Danny finally slips into a deep sleep. Mom has taken care of Danny, so we leave the bedroom and walk out to the living room. As if the storm has brought with it some sleeping drug, Wayne and Eddie are both asleep on the couch, in front of an unwatched cartoon. Lee is also asleep in his nearby crib. If Wayne were awake earlier, when the worst of the storm was upon them, he very likely would have been yelling, "Oogie Boogie!" (His words for thunder), in that delightfully happy way he has. Now that, the storm is waning, and the soothing rain is here, it's like someone threw a hand grenade into this room (this is one of their Dad's more amusing sayings). We hear the phone ringing from the other room, so leave the living room, and cross to the area between the dining room and kitchen, where the phone sits on a small table.

Mom has just picked up the phone, uttered her greeting, and is now listening quietly. After a few seconds, Mom leans against the wall and lowers her head, "Oh no, Joan! Oh my God…"

Mom is now shaking with grief as she listens.

"What happened?"

Mom raises her head and stares out the front window at the flooded road gutters as she continues to listen. She wipes at her tears absently.

"What? No, Danny's here...just a few minutes ago..."

Silence again, then, "Oh, he was? Oh no, that's what's wrong with him. I thought he was sick from being out in the rain."

Mom listens for a while longer, replying with the occasional, "I am so sorry", and "No, I totally understand. It will take some time."

A few minutes later, Mom hangs up the phone, then goes to sit at the dining room table. She feels so sorry for Joan. First her husband dies in a car accident a few years ago, and now Emma dies from a defective heart. Mom starts to cry at the memories of sweet little Emma. She and Danny were so close. Danny and Emma would sometimes sit for hours out front, talking and staring off at the world around them. Sometimes she saw Danny and Emma holding hands, and at other times, she saw Emma laying her head on Danny's shoulder. She now thinks about Danny and his loss, and wonders how he will cope with this. He has proved to be quite resilient over the years, but this one is brutally close. She thinks about calling Buck, but he may not understand the urgency. She will wait for him to come home. She is hoping Danny sleeps for a while, and that somehow he will recover some after the rest. Mom has stopped crying and decides that she and Buck will stop by and see Joan tonight to pay their respects. She'll call Rosita to come over and watch the boys while they're gone. They can stop by the florist on the way there to get flowers. She gets up and walks to the living room, and watches her boys sleep. They are so precious...and fragile. The thought, that they can be taken away, so quickly and easily, frightens her to her core. She shoves away the thought because it is so terrible. One after another, she leans over and kisses the cheeks of her three sleeping boys, fighting the sudden urge to wake them, so she can see they are alright. She sees Inga sitting at her feet and realizes that she must have been walking with her wherever she went. It must be true that some dogs are acutely sensitive...Inga is sure picking up on something as she looks up at Mom. She linger a few moments longer and walks into the boy's room, to check on Danny. She doesn't see the mean little monster lying there now. Instead, she sees a boy, just as innocent and delicate as the other three. She walks to him and feels his forehead again (because she's a Mom) and brushes his hair with her palm. She pulls his covers up higher towards his face, then turns and leaves. She thinks about what Joan had mentioned to her on that terribly sad phone call, about having to develop pictures she had taken of Danny and Emma just last week; and that she would make sure she got a copy. Emma's Mom was apologizing about forgetting the film. All of this is so frightfully sad.

As Mom leaves the room, she is singing a tune we have to struggle to hear, and identify as Elvis Presley's, "Help Me,"

"Lord, help me walk another mile, just one more mile,
I'm tired of walkin' all alone
Lord, help me smile, just one more smile
You know, I just can't make it on my own."

Pools and Drive-Ins

It has been a busy June and now we are at the end of that month. It is 1964. Mom and Dad have decided to join the community YMCA to have a place for the family to swim.

A year ago, while at a company party at a coworker's house (all family members invited), the men were extremely generous with the beer. Somehow the conversation turned to the fact that Danny did not yet know how to swim. The teasing of Danny's Dad started. His skills as an adequate father and teacher were questioned—all in good fun, of course. Danny's Dad loves to be the center of positive attention, but does not tolerate teasing well. Once his friends saw they were getting to Danny's Dad, they turned up the teasing. One of his more inebriated friends, Fred, blurted out that he had learned how to swim by his Dad throwing him into the deep-end of a swimming pool—a sink or swim proposition. He had somehow moved his arms and legs in such a way that anyone watching that day would have thought he had a seizure—but by the "Grace of God", he made it to the edge of the pool. Everyone within hearing range of Fred (The whole backyard, since Fred is quite loud) knew that Fred was telling a tall tale. Fred had a history of telling tall tales. All women and children who believe this as a joke, laugh (this list includes Danny who loves these beer-

induced stories because the narrator is always so happy and funny). All of Fred's male coworkers laugh except one: Danny's Dad. For such a large man, he moved exceptionally fast. He was up and out of his chair, and over to where Danny was sitting within a few seconds. He scooped Danny up with his arms, and with no hesitation, threw him high into the air over the pool. Danny is so surprised; he makes no sound as he does two somersaults and a twist before doing a belly-flop in the center of the deep-end of the pool. The laughter from everyone suddenly stops as all in attendance stare stupidly at what they just witnessed. The only sound is the song, "Splishing and a splashing" coming from the turntable near the back door.

Two of Dad's friends and one of the women begin to move towards the pool, to help Danny—motivated by pure parental instinct alone. Dad freezes them in their tracks with a look (one much too serious for a party) and a raised hand (like an Indian saying, "How" in one of those old movies, but in this case means, "Wait".), as he slowly turns back to look at his son. When Danny hit the water, he kept on going and ends up several feet under. By thrashing his arms in an almost-dog-paddle, he got his face above water to take a breath. His legs aren't kicking together, but in a random fluttering, so he is spinning in a circle. Mom, who has been in the house visiting with their hostess June, exits out the back door. To Mom, what she thinks she sees is Danny drowning in the pool, and everyone else letting him do it.

Mom screams, "What are you doing? Someone save him!"

From Dad, "He's learning how to swim. Leave him alone."

Mom is moving towards the side of the pool. Danny is still lurching in circles and he has the wild and frightened look of an animal caught in the same situation.

Dad has moved to the opposite side of the pool and is saying to Danny, "Kick your legs at the same time. Reach your hands out away from you...like this."

Dad is totally oblivious to anyone around him. In his mind, there is just, "Him and his son". He keeps talking and demonstrating. The adults look at each other, and some are inching towards the pool. No matter what control Dad has, someone will jump into the pool at any moment. Mom has walked around and is ready to do just that. Danny sinks under the water to where only his face is above, and he is starting to tire—his kicks and strokes are slower, and less frequent.

Dad adopts a new tactic, "You better quit messing around and start swimming! If I have to come in after you, I'm going to kick your butt!"

Mom says, "That's enough! You've had your fun! Get him out now!"

She starts to jump in but Dad yells, "Look! He's doing it!"

Sure enough, probably from dumb luck, or threats from Dad (or divine intervention), Danny had synchronized the kicking of his feet, and was almost mimicking his Dad's overhand stroke he was demonstrating. He wasn't moving particularly fast, but after a half a minute, Danny grabs a hold of the side of the pool. He was planning on hanging there for a few minutes to catch his breath, but his Dad leaned over and yanked him up into his arms and was favoring everyone with his great-big-smile.

"I told you, you could do it Danny. Didn't I?" said Dad.

Danny nodded and gave his Dad a small and demure smile; not sharing in his Dad's enthusiasm. Mom grabbed Danny out of Dad's arms, and favored Dad with a disappointing look as she walked towards the house with him tightly held in her arms. Dad returned to his chair, taking a long drink from his beer, then looked up at all the men, who had still not returned to their previous cheerful selves. Dad looked at Fred and again favored him with his biggest smile (although, there was a gritting of the teeth to go along with it that time).

Dad said, "When my son, Danny, grows up and maybe he's at a pool party like this one. And, maybe he decides to tell the story about the time his Dad threw him into the deep-end of a pool to teach him how to swim."

His lips now part, but his teeth stay together, in an unusually dog-like snarl, as he leans towards Fred.

He continues, "...when he tells his story, it won't be bull crap."

For an exceptionally long few seconds, there is complete silence from everyone—like the calm before a storm—when suddenly, Dad reaches out his hand towards Fred and slaps him on the upper arm.

Dad said, "Hey! Is this a party or a funeral? Who needs another beer?"

The men near Dad (and women and kids keeping their distance), start to smile slowly at first gaining momentum as people see others loosening up. Some of the folks there had already moved away, or had started picking up their things to head home. Going against Dad was like dancing with a Pit Bull; you better let him lead.

Back in the present day, we have followed the family to the YMCA for the first time. The night manager takes the family aside and explains about all of the facilities and benefits which come with a standard membership. One of the YMCA Manager, explains the swimming classes for children to the parents, that they have introductory classes for three to five-year olds (Pike for Danny, Wayne, and Eddie), and regular classes for six and up (pollywog, guppy, minnow, fish, and flying fish), once they get old enough. The boys are all confused at these class titles, and the parents only care about the pike class…for now. Dad agrees to join the "Y", he pays the manager, and the family is finally on their way to the locker rooms, then on to the pool. The boys have a lot of experience walking in the shallow end of pools—even Olympic size—from the community pools their Mom and Dad have taken them. What makes this pool different is that instead of being twenty kids in ten square feet of water like the City pools, this pool is relatively empty (a family of four is currently camped out in the shallow end…the two young girls around Danny and Wayne's age). The deep water terrifies Danny, and it is abundantly clear from the panicked look on his face, and the tight posture of his body. He is several steps behind his family as they near the pool. Dad turns and notices Danny lagging behind, but before he can say anything, Danny puts on an enormous fake smile, and catches up with the family. By sheer determination alone, Danny lowers himself into the water, smiling, and laughing, and going through the motions as his Dad expects of him. Inside, he is as terrified as he was last year when thrown into the pool. Because they got here at the club, later than they would have liked, it doesn't seem terribly long at all before one of the staff walks towards the pool, and tells them the pool and the club are closing.

Wayne and Eddie offer the expected,

"Nooooo's",

"Ah, do we have to?"

Designed to tug at parent's heart-strings but Danny is immensely pleased to hear this news and says nothing. It is now four weeks later, and Danny, Wayne, and Eddie have been attending swimming classes twice a week, and practicing the other times they appear as a family. Danny has overcome most of his fear of the water and is doing well. He has even been able to swim in water over his head without too much fear. Wayne is also doing well and spends most of his time with Danny, getting pointers, and racing against him—short races at first—then longer every day. Eddie, for some strange reason, is highly resistant to learning how to swim on top of the water. Instead, he swims under the water (very well for one so young). Eddie will start by standing in the middle of the shallow end, then dive down and swim to the side of the pool. If he runs out of air before he reaches the edge, he stands up and takes several deep breaths, then dives down and does it again… and again…and again. Mom (who has been bringing the kids here during days), has become friends with the day lifeguard, Bobbie, who is nearly her age and experience. Mom spends her time with Bobbie and Lee, while they keep an eye on the other boys, distractedly. We, the witnesses, have been walking the perimeter of the pool, feeling something is going to happen. Eddie has strayed towards a somewhat deeper portion of the shallow end and makes a mistake in judgment when he goes under. Instead of swimming straight across the pool to the side, he has accidentally chosen a path that will take him just past the blue line that separates the shallow and deep-ends. This two foot error isn't much for an adult, but for a small child, the addition of an extra foot in water depth, is significant. We watch Eddie's silhouette as he swims several feet below the water. Mom and Bobbie are in the middle of a conversation, and even though Bobbie periodically scans the pool for trouble, from her vantage point, she doesn't see what is going on. Danny and Wayne have just finished a race and are walking towards the steps at the foot of the pool, so they can get out and lie on the deck to dry off, This is a thing they love to do during the summer, when after they get wet from playing in a sprinkler, they run to the hot sidewalk, and using the water on their bodies as a heat shield, they stretch out with cries of pleasure as the heat leeches away the cold. Eddie is only a foot away from the edge of the pool when he realizes he is out of air (the fact he hasn't reached the wall yet, confuses him, not understanding that his direction has increased the distance). Eddie hasn't been swimming for long, but the few things he does know, he does well; like knowing that just a few beats after his feet hit the bottom, he will be taking a whopping breath. When his feet keep going past the rehearsed depth, he realizes his head is still under water, but his just-learned reflexes have already been set in motion…he takes a deep breath. Since he hasn't learned how to swim on the surface—has taken a peculiar pride in being an underwater-only swimmer—he doesn't succeed in swimming to the surface. Wayne is out of the pool, and starting to lie down, and Danny is on the second step, when he has a remarkably strong feeling that he needs to turn around. He spins and quickly scans the pool and doesn't see Eddie. He looks over at his Mom's area, but Eddie isn't there. Danny looks back in the pool and sees that the pool is a little darker than it should be just past the middle and over towards the right edge. Danny says nothing, but is immediately on the move, running and swimming as fast as he can towards the shape under the water. As he nears the place in the water, he dives under, and now comes face to face with Eddie. His eyes are wide and wild, his arms and legs are still kicking ineffectually in random directions. Danny grabs him under his arms and begins to swim and kick towards the surface and the edge. Danny reaches again and again with his searching right hand for the upper part of the wall, coming up short over and over. Finally, he grabs the edge, and pulls himself up, raising Eddie's face up out of the water, where he immediately starts to choke and cough, sucking in vast lung-full's of air. Danny looks back over towards his Mom to scream for help, but Bobbie and his Mom are already running towards them.

    Bobbie is particularly upset, saying, "Oh my God! How could I have not been watching? I am so sorry…I am so sorry."

    She reaches down and pulls Eddie out of Danny's arms. She walks quickly with the child to the nearest chaise lounge and lays him down on his side as he continues to cough up water.

Bobbie starts thumping his back while rocking him gently, the whole time talking gently to him.

She says, "Get it all out. That's it. Get it all out. I am so sorry," she says as she once again apologizes to Mom.

Mom is shaking her head and says, "No, I wasn't paying attention either. It was my fault too. You're the lifeguard, and I was distracting you."

Eddie finally starts breathing more easily and has stopped coughing, but Bobbie keeps thumping his back, and rocking him. Mom stands up and looks at Danny who is now standing there quietly watching.

She says with admiration creeping into her voice, "You just saved your brother's life Danny."

"You sure did! That was amazing Danny. I may not have been there in time," adds Bobbie, a tear running down her cheek and a waver in her voice.

Danny looks back at them uncomfortably and allows himself a small smile; more to get their attention off of him. Danny sees Wayne sits on a nearby chair, so goes over to join him, plopping down into the chair next to his. Danny looks extremely tired and doesn't resemble the boy he was just five minutes before; the one who was swimming, and racing, and laughing, and in no hurry to leave here. Now Danny wants to go home more than anything and has no interest in going back in the pool.

He is mightily relieved, when after a few more minutes, his Mom announces, "I think we need to head home, Bobbie."

Mom hugs Bobbie, who is still highly emotional at what almost happened. Bobbie can think of nothing more tragic than the death of a child on her hands, and wonders for the first time, if she wants to be a lifeguard any longer. Eddie is now standing—a little wobbly—and they all shuffle towards the locker rooms, tired-looking like they have just finished a marathon.

2

Several weeks later, with the heat of the approaching summer flirting with the boys and visions of sprinklers and pools and ice cream cones dancing in their imaginations, Danny and Wayne once again become partners. They wake up early and are out of the house before eating breakfast, with only one trick needed to ditch Eddie. They told Eddie, that they were going out in the back yard but would only be a few minutes, and for him to remain there. Once they hear the back door close, Danny and Wayne quietly go out the front door. They know they will get it from Mom when they come back home for being so mean to their younger brother, but they are moving fast, and have a lot of ground to cover. Besides, Eddie is only three (both boys forget that they were more than capable travelers when they were both the same age). This is the day they have decided, to study in considerable detail all of their landmarks they know so well. They have talked for hours on where they should go, and what they should do. Their first stop is the Witches house. There is a large eucalyptus tree across the road from there, and both boys can be partially hidden while they watch the house. The car is gone again, but this fact doesn't worry the boys as much as it did last time. However, neither boy realizes the wide berth they gave to green valley. Danny's story about the inhabitants of the Witches house cruising down the paths of Green Valley, looking for victims, has affected Danny as much as it did his brothers. The boys find it is necessary to stand on something, to be able to look through the windows, because they are so high. So they have what they need to stand on, Danny sees a large rock lying at the end of the driveway, which he will pick up and bring with him.

Danny says, "Ready, set, go!"

Both boys, who have been watching for traffic, run across the road, with Danny stopping at the rock, to pick it up, but it is far too heavy. He tries pushing on it, but it is partially buried and it will not budge. Wayne is standing next to the side of the house waving at Danny, who is horribly exposed if the Witch, vampire, or monsters decide to return home. Danny gives up on the rock and runs to Wayne's side.

"We have to find something else," says Danny.

Danny runs around the corner and after a few minutes, returns with a piece of wood, two by two, and nearly four feet long. Danny leans the stick up against the house and instructs Wayne to use his foot to hold the bottom of the stick in place. He then tells Wayne, to hold out his hand so Danny can grab a hold of it to steady himself, as he walks up the stick to look into the window. The plan seems like a good one, except for the fact that there isn't anyone holding the top of the stick. As soon as Danny gets half-way up the stick and is reaching for the window sill, the top of the stick starts to move. Danny senses it going and reaches high, grabbing the sill, just as the stick falls. He hangs there, then swings up his other arm, then pulls himself up to look into the window. He sees a room full of old stuff; like at his Great Aunts and Uncles homes. There are paisley designs on the furniture, a crystal lamp on one table, and a Tiffany lamp on another. The room has a polished wooden floor, with a large Persian rug in the middle. Some paintings of horses and men with funny hats riding them adorn the walls. Danny finally tires of holding himself up, and without any warning, drops to the ground, lands on the stick, which is still leaning against the wall, breaks it, which interrupts his fall enough that he falls, hitting his head against the house on his way down.

"Son of a bee with an itch!" Danny says (only he doesn't exactly say this phrase). This is one of his favorite phrases when adults aren't around.

"Ummmm, you are going to get in trouble for saying a bad word," responds Wayne, who never uses cuss words.

"What did you see?" Asks Wayne; not knowing what to expect.

"Just an old house; like Aunt Mary's. Do you want to see? I can try to pick you up."

"Nah, that's ok. What do we do now?"

"Let's go walk down the steps."

Wayne shakes his head because the stairs is by far the riskiest. They have a chance of getting away, if they stay up here. If they are down on the steps along the steep hillside, they will not be able to move fast enough.

"Let's go to the steps, and we can look for something, to stand on. Let's go," says Danny.

Danny walks off before getting agreement from Wayne. Wayne stands there for a few uncertain moments and almost decides to go home, but curiosity overcomes him, so he follows Danny. Wayne gets to the edge of the drop-off at the back of the yard and slows down to look over the cliff. The drop-off is 80 feet and has wooden stair-steps zigzagging down the face of the cliff all the way to the bottom. Danny is now half-way down and moving extraordinarily fast. Much too fast in Wayne's mind, since the stairs are extremely old and are creaking loudly with every step Danny takes. As Wayne watches, he can also see parts of the stairs swaying with Danny's weight.

Before he knows it, Danny is at the bottom and is yelling up at Wayne, "Come on! What are you, a chicken?"

Danny has called Wayne much worse, so this doesn't motivate him. However, the sudden thought of the witch, the vampire, and the monsters getting home and seeing him standing here, does. Wayne starts fast but, the swaying of the first platform unsettles him, to the point of freezing up. Wayne falls down to his knees gripping the railing as tight as he can.

Danny is watching Wayne's progress…or lack thereof, and grows impatient, "For Pete's sake, I haven't got all day! I'm going to go on without you."

Wayne knows he will never hear the end of this if he stops or retreats now, so he steel's himself and then continues. Danny doesn't wear a watch, but loves to act as if he does. As Wayne descends the stairs, Danny looks at his imaginary watch in exasperation, shaking his head, and stomping his foot. He tries to be as exaggerated as he can, then he adds pacing to his répertoire as Wayne nears the bottom. Once at the bottom, they examine the top of the cliff, fully expecting to see hideous faces looking down at them, and neither boy being able to escape.

Danny says, "Just to be safe, you watch up at the top, while I look for a hole in the fence."

Wayne looks skyward, periodically glancing at Danny, to make sure he was still there. Danny methodically tests the fence as he walks about fifty feet in each direction. There is no hole to be found anywhere. Now Danny turns his attention to the hillside itself, and with the same meticulous attention, looks about 50 feet in each direction, about twenty feet up.

"Nothing," Danny finally declares.

Wayne turns and does a quick scan of his own and which satisfies him that his brother isn't lying. They both go to where they are standing shoulder to shoulder looking up the stairs towards the top.

"You go first," says Danny.

"No, you go first," says Wayne.

Both boys look at each other and without saying so; know what the other boy is thinking, "If they climb back up the stairs, who knows what will be waiting for them." They won't dwell on the fact that neither one of them thought the return trip through, beforehand.

"Let's go down to the bridge and see if we can climb out there," says Danny

"Yes," Wayne agrees with total relief in his voice.

Once at the bridge, the boys discover that their tree-climbing skills serve them well with cliff-climbing too. The cliff is far easier to climb than they suspected, and they are soon at the top.

3

They come out near Mount Vernon and know that during the day like this, without their parents nearby, they are much more likely to be captured by well-meaning adults who think they have no business being out here. During previous visits, they have learned to avoid these adults at all times, or their adventures will be over. They decide to cut across the college campus, to go to just across the street from the Drive-in. For some strange reason, the boys are almost invisible on campus. And if some adult actually looks at them, they know how to use the well known bushes, and trees to their advantage in escaping their chasers. The best trick they have is to walk up behind a group of people and walk so close to them, to other people, they look as if they are with them. They are in luck since it is in between class; there are more people to provide cover. They move quickly and come to one of their favorite hiding places; a hedge in front of the main administration building which faces Mount Vernon. From the shadows beneath the hedge, they are across the street from the Drive-in Theater that their Dad takes them to every other Friday night. The giant movie screen perches on top of a twenty-foot hill, and the hill has caves. There aren't many things that fascinate the boys more than caves, and every time their Dad drives into the entrance to the Drive-In, to the right of the caves, Danny and Wayne strain with their faces pushed up against the backseat window to get a better look at them. Mount Vernon is the problem. They know they would have trouble getting across this busy highway without getting run over, or an adult capturing them. As they sit in the shadows, they throw out ideas, and then think about whether they will work. So far, they have decided they need to go as soon as it gets dark when people are in their homes, and the boys will have the cover of darkness. They still need to worry about Mount Vernon. Young boys soon tire of too much thinking, so they decide to move on to their next stop on their journey. Danny and Wayne think of all of these places as unique. These are places that are so unique in some special way, they defy explanation. Green valley and the witch's house are two of these, and now their next destination is another.

4

Danny and Wayne decide to cross the college, so they come out on Hazel; decreasing the likelihood their Mom will see them. Mom is never happy when they are up and gone so early, without breakfast even. We follow these two, relaxed for once—since they hardly ever get into danger when they are together, as they quickly walk past four cross-streets to J Street, then turn right and slow down. Up on their left, is a long-visited destination. It is a 30 by 30 foot space at the back of a house, which is entirely surrounded by a fifteen foot tall pine fence. At first glance, there is no entry, which, of course grabbed

Danny and Wayne's attention, and continues to do so. The boys spent the first couple of visits walking the perimeter looking for a way in, and trying to imagine what could be so valuable that they would protect it like this. On the third visit, they discovered a door facing the house, which they had previously missed because the gap between the door and the wall was so close, it was almost invisible—and the door is the same wood as the fence. Also, what they thought was nothing noteworthy (a long bolt hanging from a metal hasp nearly six feet up), is a hasp like the one on their Grandpa's shed. The door has no handle or knob, so the boy's decide to pull it open with the hasp. The excellent news is there is a bolt instead of a lock. The unfortunate news is how do they reach it? They knew that whatever they decided to do, they better do it when there is nobody at home, so they started walking by the front of the house, figuring out the patterns of the inhabitants. After doing this for several weeks, they have learned that no-one is home on Tuesday and Thursday afternoons. They know this because they have begun asking their Mom what day it is (getting a strange look from their Mom in the process) as soon as they wake up, so they can keep track of the days. Today is a Thursday, so here they are. The boys are walking slowly, then when there is no traffic, run for the front of the fence. Wayne stays there, while Danny runs to a shed at the other side of the yard, opens the door, reaches inside, and comes back with a wooden shelf. The shelf makes Danny just tall enough to reach the bolt and remove it. The next part is a little more danger, as Danny drops the bolt on the ground, then grabs the hasp with both hands, steps off of the shelf, and places his feet on both sides of the door and pushes. The door opens, just enough for the boys, to squeeze through. What awaits them on the other side is another of those should-not-be-here items. The object is an F-86 Sabre jet, flown by American pilots during the Korean War. The boys know this because they asked their Dad questions by trying to describe what it looked like. Danny explained to Dad that he looked at pictures a friend has. He instinctively knows not to disclose too much to their Dad, or the fun will be over. The boys never get used to the power the aircraft exudes; like a coiled rattle snake ready to strike. It is silver (which blinds them if they look directly at it sometimes) except for some yellow and black stripes and other markings, which includes the alpha-numeric marking of, "FA-57" just below the tail at the back of the jet. Danny wasted no time in coming up with what the "FA" stands for.

Danny told Wayne, "It's freakin awesome. That's why they call it that."

The "57" needs no explanation. The jet is also important, because it has the same number as the one on the sidewalk in front of the giant pine tree. We can now safely add this jet to our things-that-don't-belong-here list.

Danny says, "The pilot was very good to be able to land this jet here, without wrecking."

Danny and Wayne both look up again at the clearance around the jet. Both are in awe of the skills required to accomplish this feat. It never occurs to them that the fence went up after the jet was put in place. Danny walks to the left-wing, touching the surface to make sure it isn't too hot to burn him (a mistake he doesn't want to make again), and then puts a foot on the pontoon-boat-thing that hangs below the wing, so he can climb. Without much effort, Danny is on the top of the jet, walking, sure-footed to the canopy of the cockpit. Wayne joins him, and they spend the next few minutes looking down through the glass at the wonders below. They have tried to lift the glass before, but it doesn't budge, so they have to be content to just look. The seat has no padding and individual seat belts spread across the seat from different directions. Then there are the controls, which are many—the use of each—totally escapes the boys. They know all about dials, cars have those; just not so many. They both let their imaginations run wild, thinking that they are the pilots, shooting the missiles, firing the machine guns. They have tried getting inside the jet before, without success. This time they have a plan to investigate the last possible port of entry; the big hole in the nose of the jet. The purpose of the hole is unknown to them, but maybe it allows access to the cockpit. Danny, as with most things that are dangerous—goes first. He walks out over the nose of the jet (which is too high to fall from), turns around while he gets on his hands and knees, then backs up until his feet are dangling over the edge. He should have had Wayne hold his hands, but he doesn't. He should have realized that there are no handles to hold on to (just a remarkably smooth surface), but he doesn't. As soon as Danny starts to slide, he falls. Because he slows himself a little with his hands, his feet swing into the hole…but his upper body has started to fall backwards. His tennis shoes continue to slide forward, but he is falling down just as fast. Danny thinks that he will make it into the hole, but this conclusion is fleeting as his momentum takes his upper body past the bottom edge of the hole, and then he uses his back as a fulcrum. Danny pivots on his back in a back flip, which lifts his feet out of the hole and over his head, at the same time that his head rotates towards the jet. His head misses the nose landing gear by less than an inch (which he is blissfully unaware of), as his feet gain rotational speed and touch the ground just as his body gets upright. He takes a single step but doesn't fall. Wayne saw Danny's hands pull away too soon, and knows he must have fallen, so scrambles off of the canopy where he had been sitting, and down to the wing, to see Danny standing on his feet.

"Whoa!" yells Wayne. Are you ok? That was a long way to fall."

Danny has been standing fearfully still, waiting for the pain to come. He knows from experience that when he lands on a hard surface, the pain is on its way. Danny looks up at the nose of the jet, and marvels at how high it now looks.

"Yeah, I'm OK. Just slipped, that's all. Let's get out of here."

As the boys leave the way they came in, Danny is a little more subdued.

After a half a block, Danny looks to the sky and says, "If we get something to stand on in front of the jet, we can climb to the hole, and get in that way."

Wayne, who has been kicking a stick down the street looks over at Danny, and says, "Yeah, that will work. You almost did it!"

Danny, who has found a rock to kick alongside Wayne's stick, looks over at Wayne and says, "I did, didn't I? We'll both do it next time!"

Danny smiles and punches Wayne on the shoulder as he yells, "Race you home. Last one there's a rotten egg!"

Both boys race towards home, on legs that will run forever, sucking air into lungs that will breathe forever, wearing enormous grins that will shine forever. We, the witnesses, run behind, hearing their footsteps and laughter, as they disappear into the distance.

5

It is late afternoon on that same day, and Danny and Wayne are getting terribly impatient, waiting on dark, so they can go explore the caves in front of the Drive-In. As usual, Danny and Wayne are keeping an eye on their Mom and Eddie, so when the time comes, their disappearance will be cleaner. Both boys have already extracted their bikes from beside the playhouse and moved them into the alley. Now they just need to know when the time is right. Lee suddenly starts to scream, so Mom lays him down on the floor to change him. Eddie picks this moment to try to walk by Mom, stumbles, trips on a misplaced tinker toy, then falls and bumps his head on the coffee table. This starts a full-blown fit; complete with holding of breath. With Mom totally preoccupied, Danny and Wayne jump at their chance and begin to move towards the back door.

Mom yells after them, "Don't you go far, you two! Your Dad will be home soon, and we are going to the Drive-In tonight."

Danny and Wayne hear their Mom yell something, but aren't listening very close to exactly what.

They do have the presence of mind to shout out, "OK, we will!"

Mom has a puzzled look on her face at the opposite response, but she is quickly brought back to the fact that she has her hands full, so Danny and Wayne are soon forgotten. By the time Mom has bent back down to attend to Lee, Danny and Wayne are already halfway across the yard. They go through the gate and into the alley where their bikes are still awaiting their mounts. Danny has a blue kid-size Schwinn with training wheels, and Wayne has a big bright, red Radio Flyer tricycle, where he is barely able to reach the pedals. After some effort, on the boy's part to get their bikes moving, off they go down the alley; Danny in the lead with Wayne struggling to keep up. They reach the end of the alley, and know that as they cross K Street, they will be at their most vulnerable—their Dad can choose to return home from work, or their Mom can come out in the front yard. As they previously discussed (also because of the two curbs), they dismount at the corner, and then push their bikes directly across the street. Now they have several hundred yards of open field to negotiate on the college campus, where they know they can still be seen by Mom or Dad. They keep pushing their bikes until they get to the first sidewalk, where they stop briefly to look back towards their house, and up and down the road to look for their Dad's car. All looks clear, so they mount back up and start pedaling again. Danny has previously coached Wayne that if a grown-up should approach them and wonder what he and Wayne are doing here, they are to say that their Dad goes here and is in the libary (whatever that is). Danny knows this term because his Dad used to talk about "studding at a libary" (which would be amusing to any adult who overheard this pronunciation). Both boys feel tremendously grown up now, knowing that they can stop any impediment to their quest. Surprisingly, they pass several old people—each in a hurry; holding books or satchels—but none do so much as give them a passing glance. Danny and Wayne know this campus—every twist and turn of sidewalk—so get to Mount Vernon Road while it is still light. They have planned their course carefully, because they have come out right at the caves, to the side of the Administration building. As is expected most of the time, Mount Vernon is exceptionally busy. They can see many cars and trucks backed up at the Drive-in waiting to get in to the movies.

Danny says, "Those people are lucky. I wish we were going to the Drive-In"

Wayne asks, "What's on tonight?"

It says, "Viva Las Vegas, and Kissin' Cousins". At the top, it says "Elvis."

"Oh, him; I don't like all the singing," Wayne responds.

"It's ok sometimes. I don't like the kissing," Danny says while looking at the word kissin' on the marquee.

"I like when he fights, and when he races cars and boats," continues Danny.

"Yeah," responds Wayne.

Both boys are still for a while looking for a hole in the traffic.

Finally, Danny says, "Our bikes are like motorcycles. When they see us on the bikes, it's like motorcycles, and they'll drive around us."

They sit for a few seconds longer, and then Danny drops his bike in the breakdown lane, climbs on and waits for Wayne.

As soon as they are on their bikes, Danny says, "Let's go. Don't look at the cars. Just go."

Off they go. We witnesses have been wondering what has been going through the minds of drivers as they looked over and saw these children on the sidewalk, then as they stepped into the breakdown lane. There is no wondering now as the boys are now nearly across the first lane. Cars brake and cars swerve, and a truck brakes and almost runs into the back of one of the cars but the boys keep on pedaling. They still have their heads down, but notice the fast-moving vehicles swerving around them—how could they not? Of course, they hear the screeching tires and honking horns…and the carefully chosen expletives yelled at them through open windows as these people fly by. Now the boys are across the second lane and the center of the road but don't stay at all. The drivers coming from the other way have been rubbernecking, but oddly enough, have not stopped. Danny and Wayne now enter the middle lane on the other lane of traffic and the slamming of brakes, and the swerving and screeching of tires, starts all again. The people in the first two lanes have now continued on their way. Not a single person has stopped to render aid to these wayward children. Not a single person has tried to stop or direct traffic around the boys.

Perhaps this will be a riveting story to tell their families about when they get home, "Wow! You should have seen what I saw today!"

"You should have seen these stupid kids on the highway today! What terrible parents they must have to let them out on a busy road like that!"

They will tell these stories as spectators always do; with it slanted to explain why they couldn't help:

(1) By the time I would have turned around, they would have been across the road and gone.

(2) There were already plenty of people there to help.

(3) Those kids were stupid for being out there. No way am I putting my life at risk by going out there.

Danny and Wayne, all odds against a successful crossing, finally make it to the breakdown lane, and without hesitation, haul their bikes up over the curb. Out on the street, drivers who are jolted out of their daydreams by the sudden appearance of kids on bikes—causing them to respond quickly—make it a point to scream bad wishes at the boys as they drive by, in an attempt to address the source of their heightened adrenalin-saturated heartbeats. A moment before they were as scared as they could be. Now they can cuss at the source of their pain; and just like that, they're over it, and move on. Tonight they will be angry at the boys or whoever allowed them to be out there. Shock will greet them tomorrow, as they wonder why children were out there at all. By next week, they will have largely forgotten about this episode. By next year it will be a memory that they will question whether it happened. The boys are now at the base of a steep dirt hill and can see the caves approximately ten feet above them. Excitement flows over them, as they close in on their goal. It was worth it to go through everything they did. Off to their right, the cars and trucks continue to flow into the Drive-In. There is now only maybe fifteen minutes of light left, so they have to hurry. They both climb up the bank and using their climbing skills, are soon up to the highest cave. Cars and trucks down on the street below (which have resumed normal traffic flow), have a fantastic view of the boys, and honk as they drive by. Teenager honk and wave and yell incomprehensible vocal encouragement as they fly by. Danny and Wayne are too close to their goal to be distracted now. They peer into the cave and see it is only seven or eight feet deep. They crab-walk to the entrances of the other four smaller caves and see that these are only four or five feet deep. They have been dreaming and planning for this moment for an unusually long time now, and are so depressed, they just stand there staring into the caves. In their imaginations, these caves went under the Drive-In. They have often fantasized that one cave would come up under the concession stand where they could get all the popcorn, candy, and ice cream they wanted. They thought another cave would come up at the back of the large parking lot, where they could sit back behind the cars and watch a movie. Nobody would even know they were there. They even imagined that the caves would take them down to an underground cavern with waterfalls and a pool where they can swim; a place strewn with diamonds and gold, so they can just grab what they want, and then go buy candy at the store. They have talked for hours about how the jewels and gold belong to Pirates, and how they have to be particularly careful they don't get caught while exploring down there. They believe the caverns extend all the way to the ocean.

Danny turns to Wayne and says, "Let's go over the top of the hill and see if we can get inside the movie screen. Remember the door?"

Wayne does remember the door. For some reason, there is a door at the base of the giant movie screen (at the side where most people don't notice it). Danny noticed it, as he seems to notice everything. The boys have fantasized that little people live in there, and have beds and kitchens. Their jobs are to make the screen, so the movies will show on it. Many times while watching a movie, the boys imagine they see the outline (just briefly) of one of these little people.

Ever since their Dad took them to see that Disney movie, "Darby O'Gill and the Little People", they have imagined little people in all kinds of out-of-the-way places.

"Yeah, let's go look. Maybe there is an entrance to the caves from there like you said before," says Wayne.

Then, "Hey, you Kids! Get down here now!"

Danny and Wayne stop their upward climb to look down, and see a police officer down below. His car has flashing lights and is blocking the outside lane. He is standing as close to the hill as he can get.

"Come on! Fun's over! Get down here now!"

He accentuates his last statement with a frown and a finger-pointing at his feet.

Danny whispers to Wayne, "See his gun? If we don't go down now, he'll shoot us dead!"

Wayne responds, "Then let's go down."

Danny says, "I think we can still make it over the top before he shoots us."

Wayne says, "Danny please, let's go back down. We can come back."

Danny nods at Wayne. Both boys are hugely disappointed. The caves were long forgotten, and their new quest of the door to the screen had become all-encompassing…now this setback.

"Be very careful. Don't fall," comes the voice from below.

Obviously, the officer doesn't understand the boys climbed up there in the first place, so will be able to climb down. To emphasize this point, the boys descend far too fast and are presently standing in front of the police officer. The officer tries hard to maintain his professional dignity, so has to fight the urge—to scream at, or hug—these boys.

He starts slowly, "I got a call that two young boys on tricycles were crossing Mount Vernon during rush hour, almost causing several accidents. I thought it was a joke, but now I see it wasn't. What do you have to say for yourselves?"

Danny says irritably, "I have a bicycle. He has a tricycle."

He finishes with a nod towards his brother. The police officer favors Danny with a strange look; probably wondering why this boy is worried about being so precise about the bikes, when he should be scared instead. There's also a sense the police officer has that these boys aren't in awe of him, as most kids are. He wonders if their Dad is a fellow cop, which would explain their demeanor. The officer decides not to try to say any more than is necessary. Something about the older boy makes him a little nervous.

He asks, "Where do you live?"

Danny is visibly shocked at this question. Perhaps in his mind he thought, they would be allowed to ride their bikes back across Mount Vernon, across the campus, and to home. Danny is now getting worried, and Wayne is taking his queues from Danny, so starts to feel anxious too.

"I need to know where you live, so I can take you home."

Danny imagines what will happen if they resist by taking off on their bikes, and happens to look at the gun on the police officer's hip. He will shoot them. It happens in the movies all the time.

Danny gives up and replies, "716 south K Street. The other side of the college."

"What? That's got to be at least a mile from here."

He studies the boy's faces, looking for the fabrication and finds none. This situation is getting stranger by the minute, and he decides he will be glad when he drops them off safely with Mommy and Daddy.

"Get your bikes, and come here"

The police officer walks to his trunk and opens it. As each boy walks up with his bike, he lifts it into his spacious trunk.

Danny asks, "Are you going to put handcuffs on us?"

"No."

"Can you turn the siren on when we drive home?"

"No."

"Will you talk on your police radio?"

"No."

"Awwww, Man! Can you at least have the flashy lights on?"

The officer stares at Danny for a few seconds and finally relents. He says, "OK, I'll leave the flashing lights on."

This elicits an immense smile from Danny, but just an uncomfortable one from Wayne. The officer nods for the boys to climb in, after opening the back door. Wayne sits back and becomes extremely still. Danny hops around looking at everything—truly enjoying the fact he is in a police car thoroughly. The officer walks carefully to his door, stands sideways for a few seconds until passing cars go by, and then he quickly gets into the driver's seat. After starting the car, he looks in the rearview mirror and sees the youngest boy is remarkably quiet and stares out the side window. The older boy has an enormous "Hey-it's-my-Birthday" grin, and stares right back at the officer. Why this unnerves the officer, he can't exactly say. There is something peculiar, about a kid acting this way in this situation. He puts his car in gear and pulls out. He knows where K Street is, and could probably guess with some certainty where he can find 715. After all, this has been his beat for many years now. He doesn't ask for any further information from the boys, and they don't volunteer it.

He slows a few houses from their house, and Danny finally says, "We live in the third house from the corner."

The police car pulls to a stop in front of their house and out run Mom and Dad. The expression on Dad's face quashes Danny's happy mood. Dad is way beyond upset. Mom reaches the back of the car, as Dad stands off a little glaring at the car.

Mom tries to open the back door, but the officer has it locked, and he yells, "Hold on Ma'am. I'll come around."

He reaches across the backseat and pulls up the lock, and then leans the other way, gets out and moves towards his trunk, just as Mom has opened the back door and is helping the boys out of the backseat.

Mom asks, "What happened? Where were they?"

"Hold on just a second Ma'am. Let me get their bikes out first, and then I'll come around to explain things to you."

At the mention of the word "bikes", Mom turns to look at Dad, but he will not look at her. He is currently extremely busy drilling holes through the boys with his laser focus. The boys will not look at their Dad. Once both bikes are on the sidewalk, the officer shuts his trunk and comes around to face Mom and Dad, who have moved back to each other's side. The boys have decided to stand back beyond easy striking distance from their Dad.

"I am Sergeant Martinez, and I received a call while I was out on patrol that two boys on tricycles rode across Mount Vernon during rush hour, almost causing several accidents…"

Danny says sharply, "I have a bicycle. He has a tricycle."

Dad spins around and glares at Danny as he raises his hand to strike. He remembers the policeman and glances at him, deciding to drop his hand; for now.

Mom says, "What, all the way to Mount Vernon; that far?"

Dad continues to remain silent.

"Well, when I got there, I see the bikes at the foot of the hill that the Drive-In screen sits on, but no boys anywhere. I pull over and start looking around, and was a little worried that maybe they did get hit, but then I look up and there they are on the side of that hill, where those holes are."

"They're caves," Danny mumbles.

"Shut up!" Says Dad, with a slap to Danny's shoulder—evidently he is not as far out of reach as Danny thought.

The officer stares at this exchange, studying both parties with a practiced eye, and says nothing.

"So, the boys are at the caves—no above—the caves. It looked as if they were going higher to the top, when I yelled at them, to come down."

Dad continues to keep quiet, except for the previous outburst.

Mom asks to no one in particular, "Why would they go there? What is there? I don't understand."

"I'm afraid I don't have an answer to that. Maybe the boys will tell you."

The officer pulls out a small notepad from his shirt pocket and asks Mom and Dad information he will need for his report. With each new question, Dad gets angrier. Finally, the officer closes the notepad, and then puts it back into his pocket.

He says, "I have to be going now. You folks have a good evening."

Sergeant Martinez stops at the back of the trunk, then turns back to face the family.

He says, "Mr. Walker, I forgot to ask you a question."

Dad finally manages a smile and a, "Yes Sir?"

"Are you an officer of law at all or ever been in law enforcement?"

Dad is confused by this question, and it takes a few seconds for him to answer.

"No, no I'm not with the police, and never have been. Why do you ask?"

Now it's the officer's turn to hesitate, before responding.

"No real reason I guess. More of an observation on, how your boys—oldest boy really—was not intimidated by me at all. I usually see that with children of fellow policemen."

Neither Mom, nor Dad, responds. If the officer expects either boy to be surprised at what he has just shared with them, the boys aren't in the least. Sergeant Martinez nods slowly and then looks at the oldest boy. With his years of experience, he feels—he knows—he will turn out to be a bad seed. He probably already is.

"You folks have a nice evening," Sergeant Martinez says.

He nods slightly while touching his hat in a faux salute. He walks quickly to his door, climbs in, and is soon driving off. The family stands there for a few moments as they all watch the police car fade into the distance. The increasing silence is deafening, and the fear of the punishment to come has settled over the boys like a dark cloud.

"Get into the house now. Don't touch your bikes. I'm taking those away from you and locking them up. Go to your bedroom and wait for me," says Dad ominously.

Danny and Wayne don't hesitate, but do as they are told, quickly. They wait in their bedrooms for what seems an eternity, wondering what their punishment will be. They hear the footfalls of their Dad walking down the hallway towards their bedroom. He is a large man and his footsteps are loud, sounding like a countdown of some monstrous stopwatch from a parallel universe. The door opens, and there stands Dad, with belt in hand. He has already folded it in half in preparation of the punishment.

Dad asks, "Who goes first?"

Both boys say nothing, but glance at each other quickly.

"Wayne first, how's that?"

This isn't a conversation, unless we call Dad talking to his self, a conversation. He grabs Wayne by the hand, pulling it up so that Wayne is standing on his tippy toes, so it will be harder for him to fight or get away from the belt, then the belt swings. It strikes Wayne on the back of his thighs (Dad learned long ago, that whipping a child's butt didn't give them enough pain), which is intensely painful, then follows it with two more. Danny has been standing still looking down at the carpet, awaiting his turn. Danny just now realizes that Wayne is screaming and crying and wonders why he is just now hearing it.

"Danny, step up and get your punishment."

Danny steps up. He gets five whips instead of three, but deep down knows he deserves it, so will not complain. Danny learned a long time ago that his parents expect yelling and crying, or they will keep swinging until they do, so he yells and cries as expected.

Satisfied that his boys are back on the path for good, Dad now says,

"You know, we were all going to the Drive-In tonight…Elvis movies. Too bad you blew it. Your Mom and I, Eddie, and Lee are all still going to go. You and Wayne get to stay here and wait for us to get back. You were supposed to listen to your Mother and stay here until I got home!"

That fierce look is back in his eyes, as his anger renews. He grabs both boys by the shoulders and steers them out into the hall, and towards the parents' bedroom. Once they are inside, both boys stare at their Dad with identical puzzled looks.

"Oh, you're wondering why we came here? This is the only door that locks. I was thinking to myself; self, where could we possibly put the boys, where they can't get into trouble, or get out of the house? Then self answered 'this bedroom'. Lay on the bed and go to sleep if you want. After the movies, we'll come back and let you out."

Danny and Wayne go to the bed and get under the covers, as their Dad closes and locks the door. They can hear the telltale sounds of a family on the move; Eddie crying, Lee crying, Dad yelling, doors opening and closing. Then, they can hear the sounds outside as car doors are opening and closing; more crying, then an engine starting and their car driving off. Danny and Wayne had been hoping that this was just one of the tricks their Dad liked doing to teach them a lesson, but they understand this time it is no trick. The boys huddle in the middle of the bed, and everything they hear and see (think they hear, and think they see), causes them to jump and scream. A light appears in front of them on the closet door. It has defined edges and the border fluctuates and grows and shrinks. The ghost is convincing, and only ratchets up their anxiety and fear. They duck under the covers, and terror now has them in tears, as they await the attack of the ghost. The closet door opens, and their heartbeats double as they realize that not only do they have a ghost on the attack, but also some monster in the closet.

Danny and Wayne have reached the point of terror where they will soon lose control of their bodily functions, when they hear, "Danny? Wayne?"

Both boys go into a deeper terror with the realization that the ghost or monster knows their names. They are now shaking and crying harder than ever. Their covers that are their final defense are suddenly thrown off of them, and both boys stare up at a hulking shadow that looms over the bed. They are frozen with fear and both scream out in terror at the same time.

"Stop it! Why are you yelling and crying? What's wrong with you two?"

Before their eyes, the hulking monster now changes into their Dad. The door they heard open was the bedroom door, not the closet door. They still have a ghost to reckon with, so keep looking over at the closet.

"Come on, let's go to the movie. We just went driving for a while, to teach you two a lesson. Your Mom is waiting in the car with your brothers. Hurry up, and put on your pajamas, so we can get going. If we don't hurry, we'll miss the start of the first movie." Both boys sprint for their bedroom scrambling to get undressed quickly and into their pajamas. Their Dad forgives them, and all is well with the world again.

Diamonds and Ditches

It is now early July of 1964, and Mom and Dad have been getting ready for their upcoming vacation to Indiana. Danny is approaching six, Wayne is four and a half, Eddie is three, and Lee is just over one. Just as, Mom and Dad had predicted, Eddie has been officially abducted into Danny and Wayne's "Bad Boys Club". Mom often catches all three boys with their heads together, whispering softly, obviously planning their next caper. Sadly, Wayne is now just as likely to be the instigator of trouble as Danny once was, and now Eddie is showing signs of having the same tendencies. For quite a while now, only one parent at a time can leave the house to go shopping, so the other one can stay, at home, to watch the boys. This causes a problem when Mom and Dad want to make shopping decisions together. They already had the failed experiments of taking the boys into the stores with them. Both parents were trying to shop while Mom was watching Lee and trying to keep an eye on the other three boys; Dad, as usual, doesn't help much in this department. The result is Mom spending all of her time running after the boys, while clumsily dragging Lee's stroller after her. Punishment doesn't work, or work for long—not that it hasn't been tried by Dad several times—to be quickly forgotten by all three boys as soon as they get inside any store. Stores are just way too tempting to all three boys; a place to run and play, where it is easy to outrun most adults. When

Mom has finally given up chasing them down, Dad gets involved. Dad is much more committed and less distracted; since he isn't dragging Lee around with him. He knows from experience that he needs to capture Danny, and then the others will give up. Doing so, however, is always easier than it sounds. The boys are particularly adept at hiding within the clothes, and behind mannequins. The last time Dad was stalking his Sons, he got a freebie, when Eddie (who is too inexperienced at this game), stuck his head out of the clothes he was hiding behind at the wrong time and Dad pulled him out. Now, he has Eddie under his arm, carrying him like a sack of flour, while he enlists the help of some of the store's employees to perform a sweeping maneuver. Yelling out threats or promises for treats has not worked. The boys know of their Dad's quick temper and that once they push him over the edge, he doesn't come back, until he gets to take it out on the backsides of his boys. The only option Danny and Wayne have now is to extend their punishment for as long as they can. Danny is currently watching as his Dad comes down the main aisle towards him with a wriggling and crying Eddie under his arm. Wayne is hiding on the other side of the aisle from where he is. Danny moves to the backside of the clothes rack he is in, and when the time is right, sneaks out into the back aisle, where a hand clamps down on his right arm. He looks up and sees one of the store employees with a grin of satisfaction on his face.

"I got one," the employee shouts to Dad.

He drags Danny out to the main aisle and stands next to Dad.

"We have Danny and Eddie. It's time to come out Wayne," Dad says.

Dad takes a deep breath to increase the volume of his threat, when Wayne steps out into the aisle. Wayne has his head down, knowing that their punishment awaits them, once they go somewhere private. Because of these critical lessons learned, Mom and Dad have decided to try a new plan. They will leave Danny, Wayne, and Eddie in the car, while they and Lee go shopping. They will threaten the boys to stay in the car, then take their time shopping the way they want to do it—the way it should be done; with no interruptions. They put this new plan to the test that night after dinner, by going to the local White Front store.

Once inside the store, Dad goes to the window every few minutes to look out and see if the boys are behaving. He sees them sitting in their places in the back seat like perfect little gentlemen, and he decides that this is a brilliant idea. He wonders why he hadn't thought of it before. The boys are sitting in the big backseat of their Dad's blue 1956 Mercury. The back windows are rolled down so the boys get some air on this terribly hot June night. The boys have all been staring at the front window of the store and have been noticing their Dad as he walks up and glares at them. Danny notices that he is waiting longer to show up each time, and has shared this fact with his brothers. The boys may look like perfect little gentlemen from the window twenty feet away, but what their Dad does not see (or hear) is the boy's mounting anxiety.

Fighting starts out small (like it always does), with a push from Danny (right side), to Eddie (center).

"You're too hot and too close. Move over!"

Danny pushes Eddie into Wayne (left side), who promptly pushes Eddie back, into Danny…completing the pendulum movement.

This goes on for several more pushes with Eddie being the human weapon shared by Danny and Wayne, until Danny has had enough, and leans across Eddie, to hit Wayne in the arm with a, "Quit it!"

Eddie, tired of being the meat between these violent pieces of bread in this sandwich, yells out, "Stop or I'm telling Mommy and Daddy!"

Wayne has now recovered from his arm punch and without warning leans across Eddie and hits his older brother. Danny decides to escalate the hostilities by jumping across Eddie and putting Wayne in a headlock. Soon they are wrestling and punching each other, and poor Eddie has nowhere to go to get out of the way. Danny and Wayne's arms and legs are kicking everywhere (including into Eddie). Now, Eddie is screaming, and Danny and Wayne are wailing on each other. Wayne is now pushing Danny up against his door, and Danny is just about to turn the tables on his brother when all of a sudden the door opens, and he falls out on the parking lot asphalt. Before he can scramble to his feet, Dad lifts him up and sets him roughly back in his seat. Wayne has moved back to his seat and is doing his best to look as innocent as he can.

Eddie is sitting there waiting out. "They beat me up! They hit me, for no reason!"

Dad puts his right forefinger to his lips and gives the boys "The look". Eddie stops talking immediately, and Danny and Wayne know better than to say anything.

Dad says, "You were so busy fighting you never noticed me as I was watching you through the glass, or outside the car window. I am going back inside to finish shopping with your Mom, and you better not lay a finger on each other. You understand me?" All three boys nod, and he doesn't notice the look of panic—the pleading eyes that say "help me"—from Eddie…not trusting his older brothers at all. Dad walks back in, and the boys are again perfect gentlemen. Every time Dad comes to the glass, they are sitting very still.

After a few minutes, Danny turns to Wayne and says, "See this window?"

He has his right hand draped over the three or so inches of glass that is remaining up above the door (the design of these style cars). Wayne is giving him a strange look, and Eddie is still sniffling and looking at the floor.

"It's diamonds. I saw it before on a broken window at Julio's house. When it breaks, it turns into diamonds. We can buy whatever we want with diamonds."

Danny has his enormous smile now, which has always unnerved his brothers. How can Danny go from trying to kill his brothers one moment to wanting to share a fortune with them the next? Danny leans over and opens his Dad's toolbox, which is sitting in the floorboard. Despite protests from both Wayne and Eddie about how they are not to go near their Dad's tools Danny ignores them and comes out with a hammer. Danny hesitates enough, to look out through the front window, to see if Dad is there, then turns and starts breaking out the right rear window. It only takes nine hits, and all of the three inches of glass is gone.

Without hesitating, he turns around and yells, "Move!" To his brothers so he can get to the other window.

He looks for his Dad again, and when he doesn't see him, goes to work on the left rear window. It only takes him eight hits this time before his work is done.

Now with his enormous smile again, he says, "Start picking up the diamonds. I'll put this hammer back."

Danny disappears into the floorboard while Wayne and Eddie get smiles of their own, as they start picking up the diamonds from the floor and seat.

Danny stands up and says, "Some fell outside. Someone else will take them if I don't"

Danny opens the door and squats down to gather up all of the pieces, then scrambles directly behind the back of the car to the other side where he quickly gathers up the others. Every piece has gone into his two front pockets. He opens the door, climbs in, and instructs his brothers to put their gems into their pockets; which they gladly do. They scoot around to make sure they are sitting in their original positions, and then they get real still; and wait. A half hour later, out walks an exceedingly happy Mom and Dad, pushing a singularly happy Lee in his stroller. Dad has his arms full of bags for their upcoming vacation. They all walk, on the right side of the car, to get to the trunk, to put the stroller in, and when they come to the back window, freeze. Mom and Dad are both staring at ragged edges of glass that has been recently broken off. They both bend down to look through at the other window and see the same thing. Danny and Wayne look straight ahead at the seat in front of them. Eddie has a large smile from his unexpected and sudden wealth, and can't wait to tell his Mommy and Daddy about his recent prosperity.

"What the hell!" Dad bellows out, as he reaches out to touch the edges of the broken glass.

Mom warns, "Be careful Honey, you'll cut yourself!"

"This is safety glass. It can't cut me."

Dad runs around the car to the other side and feels that glass, as well. He looks on the ground for the broken glass but doesn't see any. He puts his head through the back window (causing all three boys to lean away frightened) and still sees no glass anywhere. He leans over and sees his toolbox is still shut and latched.

Furious now, with the mystery of how his windows got broken evading his understanding, Dad rips open the door and leans towards Danny, "Talk!"

He grabs hold of Danny's right arm and starts to squeeze it. Danny is now grimacing, but isn't going to say anything.

Mom says, "Honey, you're hurting him. Let go." Mom lays her hand on Dad's arm to accentuate her request.

Dad stands up, turns toward the traffic, running his hand through his hair, and ponders what to do next. He visibly takes several deep breaths, and then turns back to the open door. He leans in again, and Danny flinches back as if he is about to be hit, but the hit never comes.

"Hi Eddie. You look happy. The last time I came out here, you weren't happy at all. In fact, you were crying. Why are you happy now Son?"

Eddie's smile fades a little (with the memory of Danny's coaching him to keep quiet), but his secret is just too delicious to keep to himself, "I'm rich."

"You are? Wow, that sounds exciting. Do you have money?"

"No, I have diamonds"

Dad is as perplexed as he has ever been before. Diamonds? Then it hits him, and he looks at Eddie's pockets. There are small, irregular edged bumps in each of his pockets. Danny and Wayne both see Dad looking at Eddie's pockets, and decide to put their hands in their laps, in a futile attempt to hide their own fortune.

"Can I see some of your diamonds, Eddie? I'd sure like to see them."

Dad's smile is big, and his manner is friendly. Eddie is buying this act because of his lack of experience in dealing with Dad, but Danny and Wayne are waiting for the real Dad to show up. To Danny and Wayne's horror, Eddie is reaching into his pocket, still grinning ear to ear, and pulls out a palm-full of diamonds.

Dad reaches out and picks up one of the diamonds and studies it, "Wow Son, that's a nice diamond! Let me show your Mom, can I?"

Eddie nods happily, his passion for being rich, not waning at all. Dad turns and starts whispering to Mom. There is some anger in their argument, but the clipped tones, and the rapid whispering determines this.

Occasionally, we hear from Mom a,
"Not here",
And,
"There are people around here".

This is enough to understand the gist of the conversation. Danny and Wayne take this time to look at each other as two prisoners on death row will, when they know this is the last time they will see each other. Dad lifts out Lee and hands him to Mom, while he puts the stroller and the sacks of supplies in the trunk. He climbs into the driver's seat and starts the car. He doesn't look at or talk to anyone. As the car gets closer to home, Danny and Wayne feel more and more dread at the upcoming interrogation and punishment from their father. Because Wayne is usually there when Danny gets into trouble, he is always presumed guilty, until Dad proves him innocent. Danny and Wayne stare out their windows (what's left of them), trying desperately to think of anything else, except what happens when they get home. Eddie sits in the middle, bent forward and admiring the diamonds in his hand; holding them up to the light and looking through them as he happily sings a line which would be hilarious to Danny and Wayne under any other circumstances, "Diamonds are a girl's best friend."

2

The family has just spent five days (add to that a two-day drive there, and two days back, for a nine day vacation) outside of Lafayette, Indiana with Dad's parents, who own a 25 acre farm, with chickens, cows, and a mule. There was a hand pump mounted to the kitchen sink—with a full glass of water next to it, used to prime the pump (that the operator better remember to fill again before the water stops)—that was used to draw water from the well, an outhouse out back, and goose down beds, which completed this extraordinary experience for the boys. They even got to go out and help their Grandpa with his chores: milking the cows, gathering eggs, and calling in the cows. In California, the boys expect certain smells; sagebrush, orange blossoms, pepper trees, eucalyptus trees, and cactus flowers. In Indiana, the boys picked up on the rich and pungent smells from this part of the country, which are so new to them. It's not only the smell of the farm animals, but the smell of rotting wood in a rain-soaked forest, the smell of mildew, and the musty smell of the lazy flowing muddy creeks, like the wildcat. It's the bitter smells of ivy's, stinging nettles, and milkweed, the smell of freshly mown hay from the farmer next door, and the grass from the nearby highway. All of these smells make the boys feel more alive than they ever have before. One of the things that positively fascinated the boys was fireflies. These delightful creatures don't exist in their California, but in Indiana, they are everywhere. One night, just as the sun was going down, their Grandpa had all of the grand kids (9 in all), pile into the back of his old International Harvester truck, and he drove out into the far reaches of their property, where there weren't merely dozens, or hundreds of fireflies, but thousands (millions in the children's minds). They were each handed a mason jar, with quick instructions on how to obtain their magical prizes—but be careful to not fall, and break your jar, and cut yourself. As is true with all magical events, some events can only sweep up young children; the kids get totally lost in the moment. They are aware of the flashing bugs they are chasing, and more aware of their rapidly filling jar of fireflies, and vaguely aware of the laughter of their brothers and cousins, but that is all. Time and place cease to exist. Where they are, when they are, have no bearing whatsoever. They are so lost in this single activity, that it is a shock when their Grandpa starts to yell at them that it's time to jump into the truck and head back, that they have collected enough fireflies. During the drive back, all of the kids in the back, do their best to try to count the fireflies they have in their own jar, so they can try to outdo the others. Once they get back, they give all the kids a while to show off their prizes, and then the adults tell the kids to release them back into the wild.

    A few of the children protested, but a well placed guilt salvo from one of the parents like, "These are firefly children, who were on their way home to their Mommy and Daddy when you caught them. You better let them go so they can go home."

This usually worked for all grand kids except the Walker boys. A stern look from their Dad did the trick for them. This way of life was so different to the boys because they don't yet understand that progress was happening exceedingly slowly across the country, and in remote parts of Indiana, it was slow indeed. As they crossed through Illinois, Iowa, Nebraska, Wyoming, then Utah (they took the southern route through Dallas on the way there, the northern on the way back), the boys talked almost nonstop about how much fun they had at their Grandparents house. They loved the fact that they got to "Go native", by running barefoot and shirtless everywhere as their cousins did. They also loved that all they had to do was, go down a hill, to get to their Aunt and Uncle, and six more cousin's house. They thought it was uncommonly neat that almost everything they ate, and drank, came from the farm. They had just left Lincoln Nebraska behind, and all of the older boys are asleep. The road is straight and long, with just a few other cars visible, and the only sound is the hum of the tires from the family's new all-white 1962 Chevy Bel Aire Station Wagon on the road. For hundreds of miles, Dad had been threatening to pull over to beat his kids, because, for some strange reason, Danny, Wayne, and Eddie had all teamed up to terrorize Lee. Since this had never happened before, Mom and Dad were still debating on how to deal with this. Dad planned on putting the "Fear of God" back into them once they stop.

Just as Mom and Dad are beginning to relax with the unexpected quiet, Eddie yells out, "Ouch! Quit it!"

Mom spins in her seat, expecting to catch Danny or Wayne going after Eddie, but they are both sound asleep; or pretending to be. Danny is leaning against the left door, then Eddie, then Lee in his seat, then finally Wayne at the other door. Eddie was still grimacing, but as she watched him, he drifted off to sleep. As is usual, Lee had a large grin as he sucked on his bottle with one hand, and admired the movement of his other hand; as if noticing it for the first time.

Mom turned back around in her seat, and gave her report, "I think Danny turned in his sleep and bumped Eddie."

Dad nodded as if the report was satisfactory then Wayne yelled out, "Ow! Stop!"

Mom spun again, and again, saw no movement except from Wayne, as he looked around before going back to sleep.

"What the Heck? I don't understand, "said Mom.

"What? What's going on? Do I have to pull the car over?" Dad asked, predictably.

"No, hold on, I have an idea," responded Mom.

She turned in her seat slowly and leaned over near the door, then lifted her head until she could barely see over the seat.

She didn't have to wait long to see Lee leaning way left out of his seat, with his bottle extended, then hit Danny on the head. "What the," Danny yelled.

Danny's eyes flew open, but he isn't in time to catch Lee repositioning his body back in his seat, then looking forward as he is pondering some mathematical equation.

Danny leaned forward, looked at his brothers, and then must have decided it was Eddie because before Mom could say anything, he swung his right elbow into Eddie's stomach. Eddie started to cry, Danny tried to act like it wasn't him by feigning sleep, and Wayne's eyes fluttered open, and then closed again.

Dad said, "That's it; I'm pulling over, and beating some butt!"

Mom said, "Wait. Let me explain what's going on."

She did, and Dad listened. While he listened, he looked in his rearview mirror at Lee with admiration. Every once in a while during Mom's story, Dad muttered, "Way to go Lee."

Just outside of Provo Utah, after a terribly long day of driving, the family stops. They have driven over 1,500 miles since their start yesterday morning. The road and sleep (and cramped quarters), tires everyone. Dad sees a sign for available cabins, just as they round a bend and decides to stay. It is a grouping of bungalow's scattered over a spacious plot, with towering carefully placed hedges between each one, adding to the illusion of isolation. They pay at the front office, and then drive over to where the cabin's path is. The fact that it is necessary to walk to the cabins is also a lovely feature. As they all climb out of the car and stretch, the crisp mountain air fills their lungs. There is no pollution here at all and the family appreciates this fact after breathing the air at home for so long. There is the strong smell of pine in the air, improved by the smell of a recent heavy rain which makes the air much more clean and rich. A refreshing breeze raises goose bumps on their exposed arms, causing Mom and the boys to rub their arms furiously (Dad seems to be immune to the chill).

Dad takes in a large breath and seems to double in size to the boys, before he lets it out in a long sigh, then turns to the family with a broad smile and says, "I think I would like to live here. Wouldn't you?"

The boys are smiling and nodding, loving the thought of all the hills, mountains, and trees, but Mom keeps her opinion to herself. Buck wouldn't be able to find as high a paying job, and they would be leaving behind all of her family. Besides, Buck has said the same thing almost every place they have stopped, so she isn't worried. The parking lot still has puddles from the recent downpour, but the rain is well past them now. Danny and Wayne go to the trunk and assume their positions as small suitcase carriers. Dad joins them and gives them a smile for remembering their duties. Mom has unloaded Eddie; who wanders off to investigate the absorbency of his tennis shoe leather with the nearest puddle—while she helps Lee out of the car.

"It's a lot cooler here than I imagined. I'm glad I remembered to pack warm clothes," says Mom.

Dad responds, "I'll unload all of the suitcases then. We got it handled, right Men?"

Danny and Wayne reply with generous smiling faces, "Yes Sir!"

Mom walks Eddie (who is eyeing every puddle with interest), and Lee down the path to find the cabin. Dad loads the small suitcases and bags, and finally some jackets into Danny and Wayne's arms. Once satisfied that they will not drop anything, he shuts the car hatch then simply lifts two-hundred pounds of suitcases without even struggling. They walk down the main path until it splits (and they have no idea, which way to go), when Mom appears at the curve down the left path. These paths are not straight so everyone is memorizing where they go.

They walk up on the front porch of their cabin, and Danny says, "It looks like the Hansel and Gretel Witches House. It's as if you can eat it."

"It's called Bavarian style. Many houses in Germany are like this," answers Dad.

Thinking of the curvy route to get here, Danny says, "Maybe we should have left breadcrumbs on the path between the car and here."

Danny laughs nervously but his Dad and Wayne don't join him but look around instead. Perhaps the earlier attraction of these cabins' isolation is now seen in an entirely different light. Danny still thinks that dropping bread crumbs is a terrific idea. They go inside the cabin and see that there are two bedrooms with two beds in each, and one large kitchen and living room combined area. There is even a fireplace, which excites everyone. Dad says that maybe they can roast marshmallows later. All the boys want to do is run…to explore their surroundings, for being in the car for so long. Besides, they have a history of exploring their surroundings when on vacations, hearing the "Don't go far" message every time. Mom helps to get Eddie and Lee into their heavy jackets as Danny and Wayne take care of that on their own.

Dad has disappeared back into the bathroom, so Mom looks at her watch, and then says, "Go outside, and don't lose sight of the cabin."

Danny and Wayne stand at the door with their hands on the knob, staring intently at their Mom, and answering clearly in the affirmative. Eddie is watching Danny and Wayne (and probably dreaming of un-kicked puddles) and says "Yes" after he hears his brothers say it. Lee is staring off at the broom closet for some unknown reason and doesn't follow until Mom turns him towards the door and gives him a push.

"Danny, you make sure you and Wayne keep an eye on your little brothers. OK?"

Danny says what is expected of him, and he means it this time, "Yes Ma'am."

"Be close, because your Dad wants to take you guys hiking. OK?"

The boys all shout yes as they file out of the cabin. None of the boys hear what their Mom just said, since, in their minds, they were already running through faraway places. They pause for a few seconds on the edge of the porch and take deep breaths, all with the same content smiles on their faces, then they are off the porch and down the first path they encounter. It seems that the air has gotten a little colder during just the few minutes they have been inside. These stupid hedges are blocking the sight of their surroundings. Danny leads the group from cabin to cabin, around twisty curves until they emerge from the hedges and can see wide open spaces—eager to be explored—in the distance. They can see a line of pines up ahead with a large meadow past that, then a larger forest past that which runs across hills stair-stepping up to some mountains in the distance. Shrouding the peaks of those mountains is the long-departed storm, with sporadic lightning taking pictures of lonely pines, and rocky cliffs. During those brief instances, everything is revealed (mostly trees and fascinating rock formations). Then, the grays, dark blues, and purples, move back in, as the bright light fades. The idea that there are things up there, that the lightning doesn't reveal—things that remain mysteriously hidden—like the dark, sleepy woods where Rip Van Winkle fell asleep, and bowling elves awaken him, is tremendously powerful on the psyche of young, adventurous minds. The rolling distant thunder echoes through the hills; stumbling and falling over each other; sounding more like distant memories of their former selves. In the boy's minds, there must be the largest elf bowling tournament ever, where the lightning continues to flash with the strike of the balls on pins, and the thunder signifying the falling of those pins. All four boys stare at the lightning show in fascination, and their bodies are frozen by their extreme focus.

"Look at that…" Danny says with genuine awe in his voice.

"I wish we had time to go up there," He continues.

Wayne says, "Eddie and Lee will slow us down."

Danny is genuinely torn now on whether he should make a run for the mountain peaks in the distance by himself. Maybe, if he runs the whole way, he can catch up with the storm; or the bowling tournament. He can make Wayne stay with Eddie and Lee. Danny feels that wanderer's pull so hard right now that he hates that they will just spend the night here, then get on the road to home again early tomorrow morning. This area is so beautiful…so wonderful…he is longing to see more of it; not just what they can see through the side-window of their car. He finally decides that walking out into the meadow a little will not hurt anything. They pass through the row of pines and come to an irrigation ditch, which is approximately ten feet wide, and so swollen with water from the recent rain, it has almost overrun its banks. As they near the water, Danny halts his brothers by holding up his hand. The grass is long here and still wet from the recent rain. They feel that their shoes and pants are already soaked through, and look down to confirm their suspicions. Oh well, he thinks.

Danny says, "Eddie and Lee stay back from the water, so you don't fall in."

Satisfied he has done his duty in acting like his Dad Danny finds a stick which will be his pretend-boat and tosses it into the water, running after it as it bounces and turns, and drifts through the rapids. It isn't hard to imagine a little boy at the helm of a normal sized raft holding on for dear life. Wayne grabs his boat and throws it in, running after Danny. Eddie grabs a rock and throws his in, which quickly sinks. Not upset by this outcome, Eddie picks up a stick and tosses his in, running after it. Lee bends down to touch the ground (not realizing that the object of the game is to find a stick), loses his balance then promptly falls head-first into the water. Danny and Wayne, who are maybe twenty yards downstream, hear the mighty splash, and cries of Lee as he spins in the middle of the fast-moving water, and is coming towards them exceptionally fast. Danny leans over to try to grab Lee as he floats by, but he is just out of reach.

Danny yells, "I'm going to go get Dad!"

He sprints towards the row of pines, and their cabin beyond. We, the witnesses stay with Wayne, who is running ahead of Lee towards a bridge, fifty yards in the distance. The bridge is barely high enough to clear the water, but is more of a walkway for pedestrian traffic. Wayne gets to the bridge and without hesitation, lay's down on his stomach, then inches forward so his hands almost reach the water. Wayne goes entirely still as he watches Lee's rapid approach. It is only a few seconds he has to wait, but it seems like an eternity. Lee is still spinning wildly, and every time he faces downstream, Wayne can see his wide open, wild-looking eyes. Lee can't touch the bottom of the ditch with his feet, and the only thing keeping him afloat this long in the freezing water is his heavy coat. This is one of those moments in life when a person only has one shot...there are no second chances. At the exact right moment, Wayne reaches down with both hands and grabs Lee by his coat. Immediately, the force of the water which is trying desperately to push Lee downstream, takes Lee under the bridge just enough that Wayne starts to flip over and go into the water with him. To keep from falling in, Wayne releases his left hand, and quickly grabs hold of the end of a wooden plank. He reaches back with his feet, trying to hook them on anything he can, but there is nothing there. Wayne now tries to pull Lee out of the water again, and this time, he almost loses his grip with his right hand completely. He lets out a cry of frustration, and then looks off into the distance where Danny disappeared, hoping to see his Dad running towards him, but only sees Eddie standing near the stream and path where they came out, looking back at him and Lee.

He hopes Eddie doesn't do anything stupid and fall in too, or he will be in real trouble then. Just to be sure, Wayne yells at Eddie, "Stay where you are! Don't move!"

Wayne's right hand that is holding on to Lee has now grown numb from the cold water. He is afraid he is losing his grip, and will not even know it. Just as he has this thought, his grip loosens, which scares him so much, he almost screams out in terror. If he should let go before his Dad gets here Lee will drown; he knows in his heart that this is true.

Wayne does scream out now as the agony in his arm, shoulder, and back seizes him, and demands he let go and relax. He screams, "Oh God. Please help. Oh God, please help me."

Wayne fights the urge to re-position his feet or other hand, for fear of losing Lee. A movement in the distance catches Wayne's attention and here comes Dad at a dead run down the path with Danny right behind. Dad's enormous strides, closes the distance quickly, but to Wayne it seems like his Dad is running in slow motion. His arm is now beginning to spasm, with flashes of pain running up over his shoulder, up his neck, and all the way down his back. Lee has been swaying in the current, and every time there is a harder pull than usual, Wayne thinks he has finally lost him, and he will look down in dismay. This has now happened at least ten times, and now—as if thinking of it has caused it to happen—he feels Lee slipping again, and to his horror sees it is happening this time. Against his strength of will, his body has finally given out. Lee's jacket catches on Wayne's curled and useless finger for just a moment longer as Wayne yells out in a scream of desperation. Lee has locked eyes with Wayne now, and the terror that had previously overwhelmed him, and been so evident on his face now changes into acceptance of his fate. A small farewell smile—one that says, thanks for trying—starts to appear on his face, and then...Dad's hand swoops down, and grabs the fabric of Lee's jacket where Wayne has just been holding and in one fluid motion, lifts Lee out of the water, and sets him on the bridge. Wayne collapses where he is, in total exhaustion, and now a wave of pain greater than what he has ever experienced grabs a hold of him for ten more agonizing seconds (worse than a charley horse he had one night), before finally relaxing.

From far away, Mom is yelling as she runs towards them, "What happened? Is Lee alright?"

To keep Eddie from being the next child to fall in, Mom slows just enough to take Eddie's hand as she goes by. She gets to the bridge, but decides not to walk out.

She asks Dad again, "What happened?"

Mom pauses here, looking around and hoping what she sees will make sense. It doesn't.

Mom says, "Hand Lee to me, so I can dry him off."

As Dad hands him to her, Lee is crying, which is such a rare event, the whole family stares at him for a few seconds in shock. She starts to strip him out of his waterlogged jacket, and wrap blankets around him, while Dad tells Mom everything that he saw; including the heroic effort by Wayne in holding Lee for so long against such a strong current. Wayne is now sitting up and rubbing his arm.

Wayne says, "I knew I had to grab him or he'd be gone forever. He'd go down the hole."

Everyone turns at the same time and looks at where Wayne looks. On the other side, of the bridge, the entire contents of the ditch go into a pipe—gurgling and churning; that disappears under the road.

Mom and Dad say in unison, "Oh my God!"

Dad turns to Danny and says, "Son, run up over that hill and see how far you have to go before the pipe and the water comes up again. You understand what I'm asking you?"

Danny is nodding and takes off running.

He goes over the hill for a few minutes before he returns, "It doesn't come back up. I saw a big field and some hills, but no water."

The magnitude of this realization is overwhelming to everyone.

Dad takes Lee from Mom and says, "Let's head back."

Wayne is now walking off the bridge, favoring his arm, as Dad lays his free hand on Wayne's shoulder and says, "That was awesome Wayne. That was impossible for you to hold him for as long as you did…but you did it. How's that arm doing? Thanks for coming to get me Danny. It looks as if I was just in time."

He favors both boys with his biggest smile and rubs a hand in their hair. This isn't the first time this family has faced death and won. They march single file with Dad carrying Lee in the front, then Danny, then Wayne, then Mom holding Eddie's hand in the rear. At any other time, it would have been interesting to mention they were walking just like the Lost Boys did—in single file—on Peter Pan, when they were playing "Following the Leader". Now, they are just exhausted, from another close call.

Somewhere along the path, Dad says, "And to think that after I had gone to the bathroom, we were all going to go walking into the hills together. If only you would have waited, as your Mom asked you to."

Danny turns to look at Wayne, and they give each other a look of disappointment; disappointment in themselves and each other. Once back at the cabin, Mom runs a warm bath to warm Lee back up. Dad sneaks out to go to a nearby mini-mart to get the makings for sandwiches: bread, mayonnaise, mustard, cheese, and bologna. He adds some chips, and some RC cola's. Not eating the steak that the gas station attendant told him about tonight, disappoints Dad, but nobody's in the mood now. He has carried everything in his arms to the counter and sees some moon pies off to the side, and some circus peanuts, so grabs an armload of both; nothing like dessert to improve everyone's mood.

As Dad walks out of the market with his bag, he is whistling, "He's got the whole world in His hands."

Magic Places

It is coming up on Danny's sixth birthday (August of 1964), and Mom and Dad have come up with a new proposal to present to the boys on how their birthday's can be celebrated.

Beginning with Danny, he will have a choice of:

(1) A large traditional backyard party with cake, ice cream, all of his friends and family and associated party favors

(2) Disneyland

(3) Universal Studios

(4) Knott's Berry Farm.

This means that there will seldom be a backyard birthday party again. Danny selects Disneyland; the plum of the choices. Danny has not yet reached the age of disbelief-in-unseen-things. From the moment, the boys assemble and are told about the choices plan, and Danny decides on Disneyland, all of the boys are excited beyond measure (except for Lee, since he has not yet been there). For the other three, it occupies every thought. Danny and Wayne talk about where they will go, and what they will do. In their minds, there are places in Disneyland which parallel their own special places:

(1) The giant pine across the road is similar to Swiss Family Robinson Treehouse,

(2) Green Valley (and the caves at the Drive-In) is similar to the caves on Tom Sawyer Island,

(3) The Witches house is similar to The Haunted Mansion,

(4) The Sabre Jet is similar to the rockets that fly way up high in Tomorrowland,

(5) The Pirate caves under the Drive-In are like Pirates of the Caribbean.

To Danny and Wayne, these similarities cannot be coincidence... there has to be a reason for the parallelism. They are firm believers that they will continue to discover new items for their "Things that don't belong here" list that will be the match—or twin—for an attraction at Disneyland. Mom threw a small celebration for Danny on his birthday, and then three days later, it is a Saturday, and the family is on their way to Anaheim. Lee is left at Uncle Neal and Aunt Ruby's, so it will be easier handling the three older boys. During the drive, Danny and Wayne spend their entire time looking off at the horizon in the distance for any sign of the Matterhorm Mountain Peak. Once the boys spot the snow-capped peak, they know they are only a few miles away, and their excitement grows. Eddie thought he saw the Matterhorn several times, but they were only false alarms. Once the family parks, entered through the front gate, and purchased the ticket books, their modus operandi is almost always the same:

(1) They will walk down Main Street together, talking about what they will do (which doesn't matter, because they always do things in the same order),

(2) They always go clock-wise, so take a left from Main street towards Frontierland; The Jungle Cruise, Swiss Family Treehouse, and then The Haunted Mansion,

(3) They continue to Adventureland; The Mark Twain Riverboat out to Tom Sawyer Island,

(4) After sailing back from the island, they will board the train and take it from Adventureland around to Tomorrowland,

(5) They arrive at Tomorrowland; Rocket to the Moon, America the Beautiful,

(6) They walk back towards Frontierland/Adventureland, through Fantasyland, and will sometimes (depending on the length of the lines), ride Mr. Toad's Wild Ride, Snow White's Scary Adventures, or the Mad Tea Party teacup ride.

EDEN FADING

Sometimes, if everyone feels like it, or they have time, they will ride the Skyway from Tomorrowland to Fantasyland, or walk there and ride the Submarine Voyage, or the Matterhorn Roller Coaster. By the time the family is walking around Tomorrowland, Danny and Wayne are already flipping through their ticket books. The best ones, the "E" tickets, let them do the best rides, so they want to make sure they have enough of those left. They always save their "A, B, and C" tickets for last, since those are usually the lame "show" tickets, where people dance and sing. Today is fearfully hot, and Mom and Dad are already starting to get tired. Not the boys; even Eddie is running with Danny and Wayne and showing no signs of tiring. They have stopped to get hamburger, and fries at an outside café…and to rest. While they eat, the family discusses the next activity they will do. Dad suggests the Rocket to The Moon ride, while he turns and points to it. Danny and Wayne see the rocket-shaped building in the distance, and their mouths drop.

Danny says, "Oh my Gosh! Yes, let's go there next. I'm done!"

Danny stands in his excitement, even gathering his trash and throwing it away in a nearby trashcan to prove his point.

Dad says, "Sit down, and wait for your Mom, and Eddie to finish their meals. We have plenty of time."

For an excruciating five more minutes, Danny and Wayne fidget; shaking their legs, twisting on the bench, and drumming their fingers. Dad comes close to getting mad at them, but somehow manages to control his temper. Finally, Mom pushes what's left of her hamburger and fries to Dad, where it is quickly eaten, and Eddie finally finishes his last fry. They are up and on the move, and are pleasantly surprised that there isn't a long line. Danny, as is his style, is asking questions of his parents at an unusually high rate.

He asks, "How many rockets do they have?"

"Does it land back here too?"

"How many times do they take off?"

"How long will we be gone?"

"Should we bring extra food with us?"

Mom and Dad show patience and answer what they can. Neither

one of them dispels the notion that this is a real rocket ship. Neither parent understands that Danny is at that "in-between" age, where he either believes something totally, or he doesn't at all…there is no gray area—just black and white. As they stand in line, Danny continues to ask his nervous questions, which causes his Mom and Dad to give him quizzical looks, but that is all. The line starts to move again, and they walk into a round room with stair-stepped stadium seating, so that everyone can see the large round glass portal in the center of the room.

Dad says, "Look up there!"

Everyone looks above and see a matching round glass portal in the center of the ceiling. Both portals are dark.

Danny is fidgeting more than ever now, and he starts with the questions again, "This is a real rocket?"

Dad winks at the man a few seats over, then turns to Danny and responds, "Sure it's real. This is Disneyland isn't it?"

This was the moment where Dad could have whispered to Danny that it was just a ride; that everything at Disneyland is make-believe; but he doesn't do this. Danny holds tightly to his armrests, as his breathing and heart rate quickens. Suddenly, they close the doors, and the pilot's voice comes on welcoming everyone aboard, and directing everyone to the two screens (above, and below). Suddenly, both screens come to life for the ground can be seen below, and a blue sky with a faded moon above. A countdown starts from someone called "Control", and then the engines start to vibrate everyone in their seats. Once the countdown reaches 3, fire starts in the lower screen from the rockets. The vibration intensifies as the countdown reaches 1, then "Take off". Danny didn't know what to expect, but the sudden deafening rumble of the engines, and the lowering of the seats from the G force was not it.

His eyes have grown wide from panic, and as the lower view-screen picture first show a receding Disneyland, then California, then Earth, Danny stands.

He yells, "We can't go to the Moon! We left Lee on earth! We have to go back! We have to go back!"

Danny is in a full-blown panic now. How could his parents have done this? They will go to the moon and will not come back for an exceptionally long time—if ever. What will Lee do without his family? All of the other people in the small theater are staring at Danny with humor; how cute that the little boy thinks this is real. Some of the people are wondering if this performance is all part of the show (to add to the realism). Even a few of the other small children, who know this is just a ride, so are more relaxed, are caught up in the intensity of Danny's declarations (and delusions), and start to whimper and cry; It appears that Danny's hysteria is contagious. Before Dad can reach Danny (and no telling what will happen then), Mom stands up, hugs Danny close, and pulls him into her lap as she regains her seat. Mom is whispering to him now, all the truths they should have shared before the ride. As Danny starts to understand what is going on—not what is in his imagination—his heart rate slows, then his breathing. Danny stares off at the below screen and looks nowhere else. Gone is his early excitement. After they land, and file out, a man walking behind them is singing, "It's over", by Roy Orbison.

Wayne's Revenge

It is a typical almost-hot early Wednesday morning in the month of July, 1965. Mom and Dad are buying a newer and larger house in Rialto, which is just a few miles away, and the family is moving to next month. Mom has been busy packing and loading up boxes for the move during the day then Dad helps at nights and on weekends (when he is around). The house they bought is a "fixer-upper", so Buck has been spending much of his time over there, replacing kitchen cabinets, doors, and fixing other things. All of the boys start the morning on this day in typical fashion: eating cold cereal while sitting around the kitchen table. Cheerios is a favorite, with Corn Flakes a close second. The boys would rather be eating Lucky Charms. Sugar Pops, or the new one that just came out; Apple Jacks. So far, Mom and Dad have been successful in not buying the sweet cereals, and the boys don't seem to know the difference. After breakfast, as is normal, the boys adjourn to the living room to watch cartoons. The argument this morning is between Peter Potamus and The Milton the Monster Show (Eddie and Wayne, respectively). Danny wants to watch Roger Ramjet, and Peter Potamus isn't even on for another hour. Peter Potamus is coming on, so Lee sits in the middle of the couch, with a smile on his face and the anticipation of his favorite show.

Lee yells, "So-So. I want to see So-So."

Lee is referring to So-So the monkey; sidekick of Peter Potamus, the purple hippopotamus. As is normal this time of morning, Mom is back in the kitchen cleaning up, and Dad is at work, and the boys have started to ratchet up the hostilities. This is the way it is almost every morning…unless the kids are sick. Mom has learned over the years that if she sits with the boys, they will just sit there like perfect little Angels, and she will not ever get any work done. The boys throw the first few punches within minutes, of Mom leaving the room. With the addition of Lee to the team, being just old enough (at just over two), to give and take a punch (although not particularly well yet), a true pecking order is now in place. Danny punches Wayne and Eddie, but not Lee (yet). Wayne punches Danny and Eddie, but not Lee (yet). Eddie punches Wayne and Lee, but not Danny (yet). As with the rules when Eddie was Lee's age, they want to do their best to keep things amongst themselves—and not involve Mom and Dad, which means Lee is off-limits to Danny and Wayne…for now. Here, is how it starts this morning:

(1) Danny punches Wayne, Wayne punches back,

(2) Danny starts to punch Wayne; Eddie is in the way, so he punches Eddie, then Wayne,

(3) Eddie punches Lee and Lee cries and starts to go tell Mom,

(4) Danny punches Eddie for punching Lee, which leaves himself wide open for a retaliatory back punch from Wayne.

Danny is off-balance from his punch to Eddie so goes down on the carpet easily. Wayne is much more experienced than he once was, and faster too, and wastes no time in sprinting for the back door. Danny has to take the time to get up off the floor, so wastes valuable time. By the time Danny gets to the backdoor, it is just closing. Mom yells some warning for whomever is slamming the back door, but Danny doesn't hear it. He is out the door and takes a gigantic leap off the back porch, then freezes. Wayne is nowhere in sight. Over the years, Wayne has become a master-of-hiding. Danny runs a few steps one way, then another…then another, stopping and listening each time. He is trying to force movement from Wayne. When Wayne hasn't been found right away, Danny goes into his "check the exits" approach. First, he runs as fast as he can to the front yard looking to see if he can catch Wayne. Then he sprints to the back yard and into the alley, where he looks again. After the alley, he starts his methodical approach, by employing a search pattern; the playhouse, the bikes at the side of the playhouse, inside the garage (even though this is off-limits to the boys). Danny stands in the center of the backyard, and then slowly rotates while he looks at everything. He looks up into the tree, scanning the branches, and sees nothing. Then it hits him that Wayne must be laying down on top of the playhouse; of course! He runs quickly to the wooden steps on the mighty Walnut tree and quickly ascends to the landing above. Danny is moving so quickly, Wayne, who has been laying on his stomach on the tree house platform surprises him, as he leaves the top of the ladder. Danny trips over Wayne and stumbles towards the opposite edge. For a few seconds, it looks as if Danny will fall out of the tree; thus, repeating the 15 foot fall Wayne took two and a half years before. Danny is just able to grab a branch and regain his balance. Wayne guessed that Danny would recover sooner, and didn't know about the close call Danny just had, so makes the wrong choice, and goes out the branch that leads to the roof of the playhouse. If he had known he had time to go back down the ladder, it would have been a better decision.

Wayne reaches the large vertical branch off the main branch (where he had previously fallen), and starts to swing out and around just as Danny yells, "I'm going to kill you! You better stop now! It's going to be worse for you if you don't stop now!"

We can sense not just anger from Danny, but puzzlement too. He can't ever figure out why Wayne always chooses to run, instead of just receiving his punishment and then they can watch cartoons. Doesn't Wayne realize his punishment is always worse, when he makes Danny work too hard? Danny is up and walking quickly out across the branch just as Wayne reaches the end that drops down to just above the playhouse roof. The hunt is drawing to a close, and that thrills Danny. Wayne has trapped himself, as there is only one way off the playhouse roof, and that is back across the branch—and Danny has that exit blocked. Danny is exhibiting one of his cocky and complex attitudes towards Wayne now as he steps out on the roof (He is angry, happy, and thrilled at the same time). Wayne has his hands up in a gesture of surrender, his eyes wide with fear. This old-familiar-monster, who is slowly moving towards him, with a wild look, an evil smile, and hands bunched into fists, is on that long-practiced mission; to kill him.

Wayne is pleading, "Danny, please, I'm scared. I want to get down, and then you can hit me. Please Danny."

"I told you to stop. You didn't stop. I told you it would be worse for you if you didn't stop. Then, you trip me and try to get me to fall from the tree."

"No. Danny, I was just hiding. It was an accident. Please Danny."

Wayne is close to the edge next to the cinder-block wall, where the bikes are stored. He senses how close he is to the edge, and stops. Danny stops too and then the evil grin spreads across his entire face. Wayne has gotten himself into quite a trap, and this pleases Danny. All he has to do is give Wayne just a little push, and he will fall the eight feet into the bikes below. While Danny looks off in another direction, he lunges forward with his hands out expecting to catch Wayne in the chest with his hands. Wayne has been watching Danny's eyes (another little trick he has learned over the years) and sees just a little twitch, telegraphing his move before he makes it. Wayne moves quickly to his right, like a Matador, and Danny—who has committed—continues towards the edge. Danny's arms are outstretched; his head turns left to look at Wayne with a look of utter astonishment, as he moves by. Even though, Danny is following his reaching arms, his forward momentum—and now downward momentum too—leaves his feet behind, and his head leaning way out (much like a ski jumper). As we and Wayne watch Danny's fall, his arms are the first to make contact with the top of the wall. The strength in Danny's arms is insufficient to stop all of the forces at work. They fold away with no slowing of his fall, or the impact to come, which happens a split second later. Danny's neck hits the corner of the wall, compresses into it, and then his head bounces back, as his legs have finally caught up with him, but continued to swing through and hit the wall. This opposite force, throws Danny's upper body backwards, where the back of his head hits the playhouse wall. A second later, his body is almost horizontal as he lands on the bikes. The handle bars, and seats dig painfully into Danny's body and the pedals below scratches his right leg as it finds a hole between the bikes, and continues on towards the ground. For a moment, he looks as if he may be impaled on some of the metal because he is arched backward over the bikes. He lays there for a few seconds motionless, suspended above the ground, and then starts to moan and fight his way upright.

Wayne looks over the edge, sees all the blood on Danny's neck and shirt, his eyes grow wide with shock, as he says, "Danny, stay there. I'll go get Mom."

Danny doesn't respond as Wayne's head disappears from view, but he finally gets his feet on the ground and starts climbing out of the bike pile. Danny is exceedingly dizzy and feels funny, but thinks he will be alright, until he notices the spreading stain of blood on his t-shirt. He moves his hand to his neck and feels lots of hot and sticky blood. He stares at his hand, and comprehension is failing him. Panic seizes him, as he realizes he has to get to his Mom quickly if he is to have any hope of surviving. He runs to the back porch on legs that are wobbly, and Wayne is already there banging on the back door. Their Mom often locks the back door, to keep the kids from running in and out when she is doing laundry…and this is one of those times. Danny is standing on the porch watching a steady-stream of blood pour on the cement, creating exceptionally large puddles, which spread into one another. He is so weak now he can't even tell Wayne to go around to the front. Danny feels like lying down and sleeping now, and is wondering why all the colors and sounds are so weird—like in a dream. He realizes that Wayne must have gone for help, and he hopes he went to the front door. Suddenly, Mom throws the back door open, and she has to fight the impulse to scream, as she sees that Danny's throat has somehow been torn open, and he is bleeding to death on the porch. She takes a deep breath to relax, then leads Danny into the house, where she lays him down in the hall, then runs to get a wet wash rag. She returns quickly and uses the wash cloth to apply pressure to the wound, which is still bleeding profusely.

She begins to apply pressure and clean off the blood to get a better idea about the extent of the damage, while she is yelling to Wayne to run next door to get Mrs. Sánchez, "Tell her to come now. Right away, do you understand?"

Wayne yells out a "Yes", and then runs out the front door. After Wayne leaves, Mom sees that the whole underside of Danny's chin is laid open, and the skin flap is hanging down over his neck, which is why she thought his throat was open. She begins to relax. Things aren't as bad as she first thought, but the blood is still flowing like a sieve, which brings her back to how serious this still is. Rosita Sánchez comes running through the front door (that Wayne had left open when he left. The back door is also open, but Mom is a little too rattled now to realize this). Rosita quickly kneels besides Mom, and takes over the chore of compressing the rag to the wound, while Mom runs to call the Doctor. Rosita talks soothingly to Danny, testing his reactions, and thinks he may be in shock. The large amount of lost blood (most of it on his t-shirt, and pants, and much leading in huge drops to the back door), frightens Rosita. She can hear Jean in the other room talking to someone, but she can't quite hear what she is saying. She hears someone talking about blood puddles, and becomes confused because she thinks it may have been her own thoughts. She thinks she is remarkably calm, but also a little dizzy, and wonders if she may be in a little shock herself. She has an unusually scary thought that Danny will die right here on the floor (How much blood has he lost? How much more can he have left?), but the thought is somehow muted. She whispers prayers now, wondering if she needs to pray for his soul, and then decides she better; just in case. Danny is unusually quiet now, and she nudges him periodically, happy to get a moan.

Mom returns, kneeling down and saying, "I just called Doctor Peterson, our family Doctor, and he said, to just drive Danny over there. I called Buck and he is coming home as fast as he can, so we can take Danny. Can you please watch the other boys? Where did all these kids come from?"

Rosita looks up and sees that there are kids everywhere—like a magical appearance; up and down the hall, sitting on the living room furniture, in the laundry room, and many just entering from the back porch. Before the children enter, they exclaim about the blood on the steps and porch, and then become quiet, as the other children already inside. All of the "inside" children have taken up positions to watch and mourn. The children are so quiet; Mom and Rosita didn't even know they are there. How could they have not seen them?

Mom says to all the children, "Go, please. It's time to go now."

She walks them out of the back door and then closes it behind them. Some have gone out through the front door and taken up sentry positions on the front sidewalk. The demeanor of these children bothers Mom. They are so somber, and how did they find out so quickly about Danny? She lifts Danny and can barely lift him. He is almost seven years old, but she thinks this may be the last time she will be able to lift and hold him like this. Rosita is holding the wash rag to Danny's chin to continue the pressure as Mom lays him down on the couch in the living room. It will be easier to tend to Danny this way; while they wait for Buck. Mom finally remembers her other three boys, and sees them all squeezed into the loveseat couch off to the side, staring on with rapt attention. Mom thinks Danny's injury is his first major one, and she wonders how it happened. She decides that she is too weary now and that the story can wait until later. She turns back to look at Danny again and the TV blasting, with volume turned all of the way up, surprise her. How could she have not noticed that before?

The TV is playing a commercial now, with that song from the Kinks: "You really got me,

"Oh, yeah, you really got me now,

You got me so I can't sleep at night."

2

It is a week later. Danny received 12 stitches in his chin, and kept hydrated with plenty of liquids for a few days, but was—at least physically—mostly unharmed. Psychologically, however, life has turned the tables on Danny, and he has learned a lesson which has kept him preoccupied with his thoughts. He isn't even mad at Wayne for being smart and quick enough to avoid the push. In fact, he admires him for what he did. For the first time in his life, the thought that he will die, scares him. Danny had never understood what it was like to be the frightened victim; instead of the other way around (he just thought the teenagers terrified him). He has always been able to stand-off and watch the action, as if he was watching a TV show; no personal attachment. For the first time, Danny is questioning why he does the things he does…why a tragic outcome has always had a certain allure—a fascination, for him. He has always thought of himself as separated from the action playing out in the scenes before him. Now, he has emotional responses to his own close call and for the past week, has been cycling through the events of his life, and re-examining them. There is no instantaneous transformation of Danny's thought process, so no miraculous changes in his behavior. This re-thinking the present, and re-examining the past will take a long time. Danny's chin has heavy bandages, and it is giving him enough pain, and restricting his movements so that his three younger brothers have a reprieve from his violence for the first time in their lives…for a while at least. A few days ago, Mom heard screaming and crying from the living room and finding Danny, off to the side and totally detached from the fighting, surprises her. Danny looked up at his Mom, gave her a sad look, managed a smile before grimacing, and then returned his attention back to the TV. The word that popped into her head was, "polite", which confused her. She then turned her attention to the other three boys who have a free-for-all wrestling match on the floor. Eddie and Lee are working together in trying to defeat Wayne, but he has no trouble in keeping them at bay. Wayne pushes Lee away then Lee falls and starts to cry. The cry is short-lived, however, as Lee (showing how tough he already is at such a young age), lets out a mighty growl as he jumps on Wayne's back, who is trying to pin down a squirming Eddie. Mom is truly depressed by what she is seeing. She has always thought that, without Danny, the other boys would behave. She realizes that the damage has already been done. Danny has successfully done his job by building this machine (with interchangeable parts) that will continue to wrestle and fight—to chase, and scream—to punch and cry, for years to come. She will have her part to play in keeping this machine going. She will feed and clothe, and bathe these machine components…again…for years to come. Mom doesn't break up the fight, but turns and goes back to sit at the small table in the kitchen. She stares out the window into the back yard, and is wondering (definitely not for the first time), why she even tries. Buck thinks she can do a better job keeping an eye on the kids. She used to bristle at comments like these, but she now accepts these jabs with a quiet futility. The boys are now at an age where they are always up to something, and the day-after-day, hour-after-hour troubles, at times, have caused her to become extremely overwhelmed…like now. Some movement outside the window catches Mom's eye, but she can't make out what she is seeing. She stands and leans towards the window glass, to get a better look, and sees that the white Crape Myrtle that Buck planted in the back yard, last month, is now in full bloom. The nursery guy told Buck it was too late in the season, and that it wouldn't bloom this year. Its white flowers cover the tree, except for the few which are fluttering to the ground because of a red cardinal that is hopping from branch to branch. She lets out a sigh of pleasure at the beauty of what she is seeing, and without being aware she is doing so, walks over to the back door, and then slowly edges out on the porch to get a better look. She realizes she is smiling, and that her former lousy mood is now gone. She feels a touch on her hand and then looks down and sees that Danny has come out beside her and has put his hand in hers. She looks down at him, and the cardinal in the tree transforms his face. She doesn't remember ever seeing him with such a beautiful smile, or to have such wonder in his eyes. If she didn't know any better, she would think he had never seen a red bird, or white tree before. Regardless of Danny's reasons, she is glad to have him back. Glad that his depression appears to be over. The wind suddenly picks up and blows through the tree's branches, causing hundreds of beautiful glowing white flowers to drift to the ground. Danny starts to giggle with enjoyment, then to laugh quietly, causing Mom to turn to him with a strange questioning look. For some reason that Mom does not understand, the tree and cardinal first transforms, but now transfigures Danny into something else. For some unknown reason, Danny has become something entirely different from his normal self, No, that's not exactly it; he has become more than his usual self, and Mom suddenly has an overpowering need to always remember this moment. She knows that life has just a few of these moments. It takes just a single word, a distraction, or a single blink to interrupt these enchanting moments. At this moment, the three wrestling boys in the house don't seem like such a terrible burden. She has a pretty wonderful life, doesn't she? She looks down at her sweet, laughing boy, and starts to laugh along. The cardinal does his part by dancing from branch to branch—branch to branch; as the flowers fall like waterfalls to the grass below.

3

A few days later, the Santa Anna winds have picked up with a vengeance, so Dad has had the marvelous idea for the whole family to go across to the college parking lot and fly kites. He stopped at the store on the way home to get some extra string and tape, and a new kite, which he tells Danny he gets to fly. The six Walker's will be sharing three kites; the new one and two old flyers. These old kites are the best ones, because they have been continually made better after each flight by: Making the tail longer, making the tail shorter, or fixing a balance problem (done by adding some extra tape to the right or left side of the wooden cross-brace). Whenever the family gets a new kite, it may look pretty, but can it fly? As soon as Dad has checked out all of the strings, kite paper, wooden braces, and tails, he signals they are ready, and off they go. It is about an hour before dark, and Mom and Dad are thankful the winds have died down some, or they may not have been able to fly the kites at all. Danny still has his bandage on his chin and is still walking slowly and carefully because he can feel the stitches getting pulled by the bandages. Dad has volunteered to pull the bandages off Danny's chin and remove the stitches himself, but Mom and Danny have both adamantly refused (Mom for sanitation reasons and Danny for reasons of pain). As always, with team exercises like this, Dad is the General and everyone else are the soldiers. Dad has Danny and Wayne hold tightly to two of the kites while he prepares and feeds out the first kite. As soon as it is at about twenty feet up, or the height that the kite flies on its own, the spool is ready to be handed to a waiting flyer. In this case, Dad reminds Eddie about the rules of not letting go of the spool, no matter what the kite does.

"If you lose it, you get to buy another one," Dad is fond of saying.

Although, how a young child could buy such an expensive item is never understood by the boys, but the threat still works. After a few minutes, Dad moves over to Danny.

Dad says with a smile, "Let's see how this kite flies. Are you ready Son?"

Danny says "yes", and manages a rare smile. The kite dances into the air, and then quickly nose-dives into the asphalt. Danny goes to retrieve the kite while rolling up the string as he walks while Dad studies the last flight in his mind.

After a few seconds, he announces, "Needs another six inches of tail. What do you think?"

Danny giggles as he yells, "That's just what I was about to say… that kite needs another six inches of tail!"

Dad takes a fake swing at Danny, while he says, "Why I ought a …"

Everyone laughs except Lee. They like it when their Dad is in a good mood.

"Oh crap," is said too loudly by Eddie as his lost spool bounces ahead of him across the parking lot, and the kite—intoxicated with its newfound freedom—is gaining altitude as fast as it can, knowing that it can be reeled back down to normal heights at any moment.

Maybe it's because Dad is such a fast runner, or maybe it's because the wind decides to let up substantially at just the right moment; more likely, it's both. Dad takes an enormous leap at the other end of the lot, and grabs the empty spool, just before it lifts too high to be reached. Dad is thinking about how he will punish Eddie once he gets back, but decides he will take care of it later. He doesn't want to ruin the fun everyone has. Eddie has been watching his Dad as he walks back and has already been preparing himself for the punishment to come. He is well past his days of holding his breath until he passes out, but he still has his frown and pout. They may not do much to stop his punishment, but he will do it. Besides, he heard the "Oh crap" thing from Danny, and will just give him up if it means saving himself. Dad gets back and continues to reel in Eddie's kite, but doesn't say anything.

Eddie is wondering what is taking so long and is particularly surprised when Dad turns to Mom and says, "Here Hon, you take your turn with this one now."

Mom gives Dad a questioning look and then looks at Eddie. Dad shakes his head in the negative, while he gives her a small smile, while he hands the spool to her than moves back to Danny. They both work together to add the extra length of tail then Danny quickly makes up for lost time by reeling out his kite to its maximum height. He starts the rhythmic pumping of the string to keep the kite where it is. Nobody likes it when the kite suddenly starts to dive back to the earth. Within a few more minutes, Wayne is launching one of the older and tested kites. Within five minutes, all three kites are dancing together high above. Mom starts to sing one of their favorite songs from Mary Poppins, which fits this moment perfectly,

"…Oh, oh, oh!
Let's go fly a kite
Up to the highest height!
Let's go fly a kite and send it soaring
Up through the atmosphere
Up where the air is clear
Oh, let's go fly a kite!"

Final Departures

We, the witnesses have seen all of this and are finally satisfied. Eden was fading for the family, but is now restored again. We nod to each other, and then walk off to the side of where the family stands. We gather in a circle and unfurl our wings. We are all over ten feet tall, wear robes of white with gold trim and belts, sandals, and have long locks of hair. Our wings spread out high and wide behind us, and we can't wait to take flight. This stay here has been a long one, but extremely necessary. Many times, a family member would have died if we had not been there to change the outcome:

1) Our invisible hands which kept the lighter fluid filled beer bottle from tipping too far…for both boys.

2) Our fingers stuck between the rope and Wayne's neck, to keep the noose from tightening too much.

3) The hands gently holding Wayne's head as he hit the ground after his fall from the tree.

4) The turn of Danny's head towards Eddie when he was drowning.

5) Holding Danny and Wayne after the branches broke at the top of the pine tree.

6) Forming a protective zone around Danny and Wayne as they traveled into traffic on their bikes.

7) The extra hands that helped Wayne support Lee, as he bobbed in the frigid water.

8) The hands that changed Danny's fall, just enough, so he would hit the wall on his chin, instead of his neck.

9) The invisible hands between Danny and Wayne's heads and the floor, when they were diving off of the tops of the cribs with the straps around their ankles, and many other interventions.

Many times, their jobs were to whisper into the boy's ears, "You don't want to hurt him. You love him. He's your brother. Think about what this will do to him."

They can't guarantee that the boy will listen to them; in fact, most of the time, Danny totally ignored these voices.

They also whispered in Mom's ears, "Everything will be alright. Look at how beautiful the world is. Look at how beautiful your children are, while they sleep."

To Dad, they whispered, "Don't swing so hard. Think about what you are about to say, before saying it. Don't punish Eddie today …fly kites and be close to God."

They have to admit that the time they have spent on Earth has been exceptionally difficult, and they are eager to be getting back close to God. The wind picks up again, and they can hear the children laughing, which draws their attention to the family they have protected over these many years. They will miss this family—despite the problems—and look forward to coming back. Just in case something should happen, two witnesses are selected to stay behind, while the others head back home. Another nod, then all witnesses but two lift off as one. To their ears only, their mighty wings make a thunderous sound with each downward stroke. Much faster than any bird, all of the airborne witnesses soon disappear.

The two remaining witnesses nod to each other, and then walk back over to the family to continue their vigil. They notice that Lee is watching them with a smile on his face. Some animals and the innocent young child can see them. Most of the time they captivate those who can see them. There are a few exceptions, where they terrify those who see them. The Sun goes behind a cloud, and a cool breeze races across the lot. They see Lee's smile turn to fear as he looks out across the parking lot. They both turn and see one of their adversaries standing far off, and watching the family. He too is over ten feet tall, but he has no light; no colors. He is made of, and surrounded by, darkness and shadow. His eyes glow with fire from hell; the only part of him not black or gray. His mighty black wings are flapping, and he is hopping up and down, as a taunt to the two protectors, The witnesses walk towards the demon, then both bow as one, and a blinding white light instantly blasts from them to their enemy, then he is gone. They stand and return to the family, not concerned about the demon; he will not return today. Once again, they can see the beauty of Eden shining in the family's faces. Once again, they can experience the breath of God, His spiritual life, emanating from their bodies. They look at Lee, and he is watching them with a huge grin. They glance once more towards heaven longingly, but then they remember their duty, and attend to the family. They know that evil is constantly on the prowl, so they will always need to be on guard.

Buck and Jean Wedding Picture, 1956

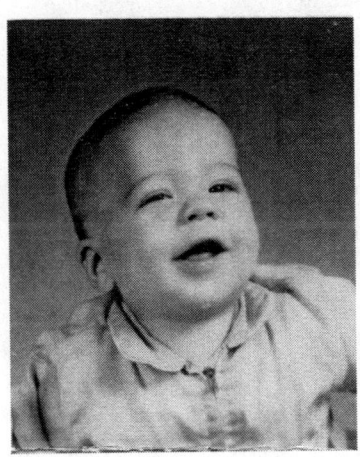

Danny, 1958

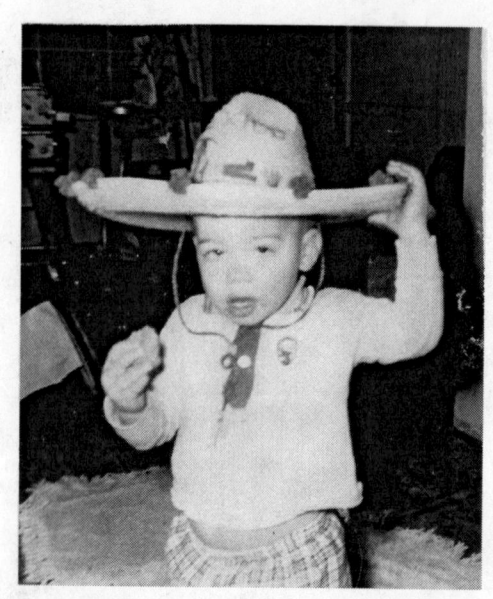

Danny, 1959

Danny and Wayne, 1960

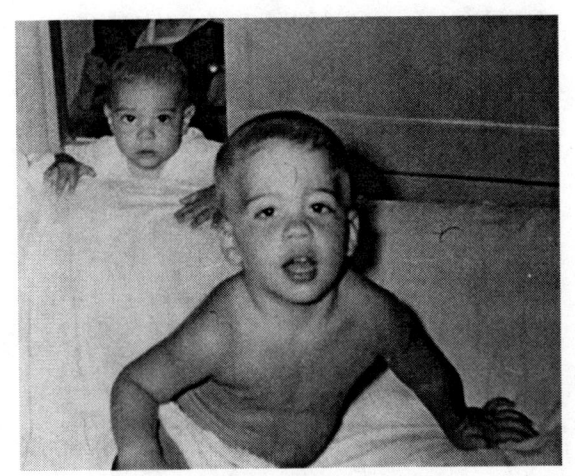

Danny and Wayne, 1961

Danny, Jean, and Buck, 1960

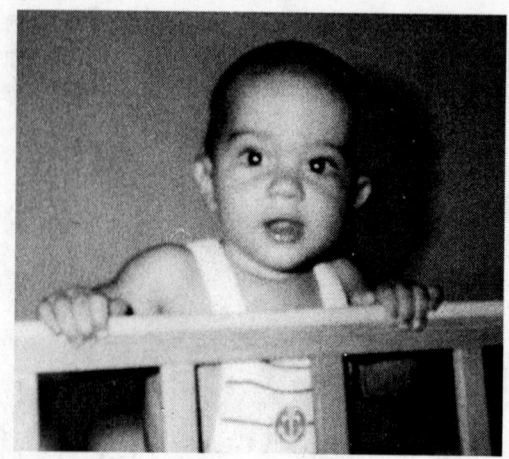

Wayne, 1961

Danny, Eddie, and Wayne, 1961

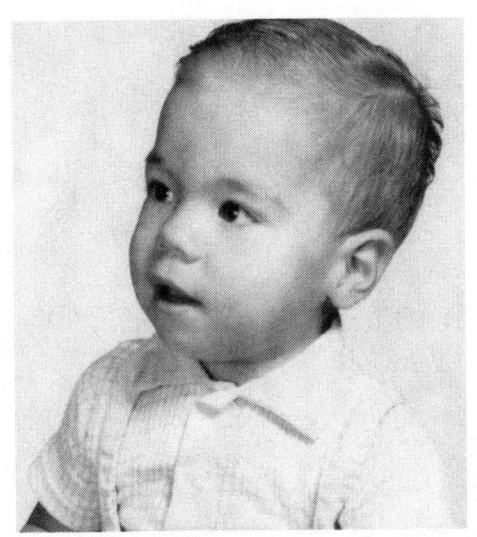

Eddie, 1963

Family, 1964